SCRIBNER
POETRY

Also by Patricia Smith

Unshuttered

Incendiary Art

Gotta Go Gotta Flow

Shoulda Been Jimi Savannah

Blood Dazzler

Teahouse of the Almighty

Janna and the Kings

Big Towns, Big Talk

Africans in America: America's Journey Through Slavery
(with Charles Johnson)

Close to Death

Life According to Motown

The Intentions *of* Thunder

New and Selected Poems

Patricia Smith

SCRIBNER

New York   Amsterdam/Antwerp   London
Toronto   Sydney/Melbourne   New Delhi

Scribner
An Imprint of Simon & Schuster, LLC
1230 Avenue of the Americas
New York, NY 10020

This book is a work of fiction. Any references to historical events, real people, or real places are used fictitiously. Other names, characters, places, and events are products of the author's imagination, and any resemblance to actual events or places or persons, living or dead, is entirely coincidental.

Always, to my teachers:

Gwendolyn Brooks
Wanda Coleman
Kwame Dawes
Annie Finch
Nikky Finney
Terrance Hayes
Marc Smith
James Taylor

Forever, to my family:

Bruce, Mikaila, Damon & The DeSilvas

Contents

Life According to Motown, 1991

She got a favorite word—*anemone*. She got a gap-toothed mama and a dead daddy and she got westside ways. She sees there's gonna be 50 poets in a blues club for five hours one winter afternoon, and since that winter afternoon is in Chicago, there's no reason not to go drink middlin' liquor and get warm and laugh at poets with all their stupid flowers growing through concrete. But they poet good like backhand slap and Gwen Brooks is there and not even a little bit of the warm comes from drinkin'. She follows Michael Warr to the Green Mill, where Marc Smith growls and guides, and that stage is hers for merely a million Sundays. She don't know line break. She don't know iamb. She don't know envoi. She knows stage and slam and people's faces when she poems and then Luis says *You got a manuscript?* because Tía Chucha and she says yes, but she doesn't have a manuscript, but she makes what she thinks a manuscript is and then it's a book.

What It's Like to Be a Black Girl (For Those of You Who Aren't)

first of all, it's being 9 years old
and feeling like you're not finished, like
your edges are wild, like there's something—
everything—wrong. it's dropping food coloring
in your eyes to make them blue and suffering
that burn in silence. it's popping a bleached
white mop head over the kinks of your hair
and primping in front of mirrors that deny
your reflection. it's finding a space between
your legs, a disturbance at your chest,
and not knowing what to do with the whistles.
it's jumping doubledutch until your legs pop,
it's sweat and vaseline and bullets, it's growing
tall and wearing a lot of white, it's smelling
blood in your breakfast, it's learning to say
fuck with grace but learning to fuck without it,
it's flame and fists and life according to motown,
it's finally having a man reach out for you
then caving in around his fingers.

Medusa

Poseidon was easier than most.
He calls himself a god,
but he fell beneath my fingers
with more shaking than any mortal.
He wept when my robe fell from my shoulders.

I made him bend his back for me,
listened to his screams break like waves.
We defiled that temple the way it *should* be defiled,
squirming and bucking our way from corner to corner.
The bitch goddess probably got a real kick out of that.
I'm sure I'll be hearing from her.

She'll give me nightmares for a week or so,
that I can handle. Or she'll turn the water
in my well into blood. I'll scream when I see it,
and that will be that. Maybe my first child
will be born with the head of a fish.
I'm not even sure it was worth it,
Poseidon pounding away at me like a madman,
losing his immortal mind because
of the way my copper skin swells in moonlight.

Now my arms smoke and itch. Hard scales
are rising on my wrists like armor. C'mon, Athena,
he was just another lay, and not a particularly
good one at that, even though he can spit steam
from his fingers! Won't touch him again. Promise.
And we didn't mean to drop to our knees
in *your* temple, but our bodies were so hot
and misaligned. It's not every day a gal

gets to sample a god, you know that.
Why are you being so rough on me?
I feel my eyes twisting, the lids crusting over
and boiling, the pupils glowing like red coals.

Athena—woman to woman,
could *you* have resisted him?
Would you have been able to wait for the proper place,
the right moment,
to jump those immortal bones?

Now my feet are tangled with hair, my ears are gone,
my back is curving and my lips have grown numb.
My garden boy
just shattered at my feet.

Dammit, Athena! Take away my father's gold!
Send me away to live with lepers! Give me a—
a pimple or two! But my *face.* To have men never
again be able to gaze at my face, growing stupid
in anticipation of that first touch, how can any woman
live like that? How can I watch their warm bodies
turn to rock when their only sin was desiring me?

All they want is to see me sweat. They just want
to touch my face and run their fingers through my—

my hair—

is it moving?

Your Man

Your man walks in on wishbone legs,
smelling like hot sauce and black pepper,
bringing me blues bound up like roses
every Thursday night 'round this time.

Your man brings me sweet bread and fried corn,
feeds me like an animal from his fingers,
tames me like an animal with his hips.
Your man comes in sweatin' that blue collar
and singin' those lies, those wash-away dreams.

I wait for his mouth, the mercy circle.
I wait. For his mouth. The mercy circle.
He neatly arranges the gasping of my skin,
leaves me gentle and crazed on a trembling bed.

Your man's lovin' leaves marks like drumbeats,
disturbances on brown skin stretched across
a circle of bone. I carved his coming
out of a mojo moonlight, out of what *you* told me
about the voodoo in his fingers.

He says *Bitch, lie still*, and I do. I do.
He says *Squeeze harder*, and I want to.
Your man hurls light against my skin
and forgets your name if that's what I need.

Yeah, your man is your man,
but he visits me sometimes,
he rocks the house sometimes,
he shakes it up sometimes,
he makes it right.
All the time.
Sometimes.

The Awakening

Since mother morning wiped clean
the chaotic slate of starlight, a hard wind
has forced the tree to beg. She bends
and splinters, bracing against the push,
her spindly fingers cramped in stretch

toward unlikely solace. All of her strains
toward the sun, which is now just a pulse
in the lightening sky, without the strength
to poke its teasing slivers of light through
the gray cloak of cloud. To move minutes,

she curls her toes into ribbons of soil.
Her skin grows wet. The lake roars in, chilling
her thick ankle, and she whistles ache
toward the skyline's bright confusion
of gray and glass. The waking sun chuckles

low in his throat as the tree's fingers freeze
and crack. Then he suddenly smacks one
of her dew-slick sides with heat. Jolted to
her toes, the tree succumbs to incessant love
as the lake recedes and the wind whispers

tomorrow.

The tree stands taller, breathes in melody,
the blessings of sun. She remembers many
things, not just the bodies flat against her,
seeking shade. She remembers lovers who
stop to scratch hopeful names into her skin.
She remembers geography's uncertain rain.
And she has a name for the moan that worries
gently in her hair.
It is called Chicago.

Sweet Daddy

62. you would have been 62.
i would have given you a roosevelt road kinda time,
an all-night jam in a twine time joint
where you could have taken over the mic
and crooned a couple

the place be all blue light
and jb air and big-legged women
giggling at the way you spit tobacco
into the sound system,
showing up some dime-store howler
with his pink car
pulled right up to the door outside

you would have been 62, and the smoke
would have bounced right off the top of your head
like good preaching
i can see you now, swirling bony hips,
growling bout if it wasn't for bad luck,
you wouldn't have no luck at all.
wasn't for bad luck
no luck at all

nobody ever accused you of walking
the paradise line
you could suck luckies
and line your mind with *rubbing* alcohol
if that's what the night called for,
but lord, you could cry foul
while bb growled lucille from the juke,
you could dance like killing roaches
and kiss those downsouth ladies
on fatback mouths. *oooowweee*, they'd say,

that sweet man sho knows how deep my well goes—
and i bet you did, daddy
i bet you did
but hey, here's to just another number,
to a man who wrote poems on the back
of cocktail napkins and brought them home
to his daughter who'd written her rhymes
under the cover of blankets
here's to a strain on the case load
here's to the fat bullet
that left its warm chamber to find you
here's to the miracles that spilled from your head
and melted into the air
like jazz

the carpet had to be destroyed. and your
collected works, on aging yellow twists of napkin

can't bring you back
bb wail and blue lucille

can't bring you back
a daughter who grew to write screams
can't bring you back

but a room

just like this one

that suddenly seems to fill with the dread odors
of whiskey and smoke
can bring you here, as close as my breathing

but the moment is hollow.
it stinks
it stinks sweet

Big Towns, Big Talk, 1992

She still don't know much because there's so much. She knows rhyme, though, 'cause she knows Motown and the Temps and the hot spot on Lake Street under the El. Weekends shelving at Guild Books, she meets Galeano and talks with Gwen again and again and later she reads with Ntozake and Olds and finds Dobyns and his tiny horrors in the thick dust of an old bookstore. She still a slammer, though, still what's onstage, still Mill and that's good or bad, a coo or a curse, depending on who thinks it. Some folks say it's a chain that needs breaking. Others say it's all, all of it, poetry. That's what she says. She wants to write horrors tiny enough to slip beneath sleep. And what begins as light veers dark. Her mother curses at a moon that didn't do nothing but rise. Olive Oyl uncloaks her wounds. The poet, flaunting newfound nerve, stalks right into the gaunt body of a skinhead and introduces herself. He doesn't even blink. He calls her nigger.

Annie Pearl Smith Discovers Moonlight

My mother, the sage of Aliceville, Alabama,
didn't believe that men had landed on the moon.
They can do anything with cameras
she hissed to anyone and everyone who'd listen,
even as moonrock crackled
beneath Neil Armstrong's puffed boot.
While the gritty film spun and rewound and we
heard the snarled static of "One small step,"
my mother pouted and sniffed
and slammed skillets into the sink.
She was *not* impressed.
After all, it was 1969, a year plump with deceit.
So many miracles
had proven mere staging for lesser dramas.

But why this elaborate prank
staged in a desert *somewhere out west,*
where she insisted the cosmic gag unfolded?
They trying to fool us.
No one argued, since she seemed near tears,
remembering the nervy deceptions of her own skin—
mirrors that swallowed too much,
men who blessed her with touch only as warning.
A woman reduced to juices, sensation and ritual,
my mother saw the stars only as signals for sleep.
She had already been promised the moon,

and heaven too. Somewhere above her head
she imagined bubble-cheeked cherubs
lining the one and only road to salvation,
angels with porcelain faces, celestial choirs
wailing gospel brown enough to warp the seams

of paradise. But for heaven to be real, it could not
be kissed,
explored,
strolled upon
or crumbled in the hands of a living man.
It could not be the 10 o'clock news,
the story above the fold,
the breathless garble of a radio "special report."

My mother had twisted her weary body into prayerful knots,
worked for twenty years in Leaf Brands Candy Company,
dipping her numb hands into vats of lumpy chocolate.
She counted out dollars with her doubled vision
just so that a heavenly seat would be plumped for her coming.
Now the moon,
the promised land's brightest bauble,
crunched plainer than sidewalk beneath ordinary feet?
And her Lord just letting it happen?

Ain't nobody mentioned God in all this, she muttered
over a hurried dinner of collards and cornbread.
That's how I know they ain't up there.
Them stars, them planets ain't ours to mess with.
The Lord woulda showed Hisself if them men
done punched a hole in my heaven.
Daddy kicked my foot beneath the table.

We nodded, we chewed, we swallowed.
Inside me, thrill unraveled.
I imagined my foot touching down on the jagged rock,
blessings moving like white light through my veins.

Annie Pearl rose from sleep that night,
tilted her face full toward a violated Eden.
My father told me how she whispered in tongues,
aching for a sign she wouldn't have to die to believe.

Now she clicks like a clock toward deliverance.
I make myself tell her that heaven still glows
wide and righteous, with a place just for her,
fashioned by that lumbering dance
of feet both human and holy.

Doin' the Louvre

Paris, December 1991
For Patricia Zamora

You're a junkie just like I am.

After we dump your husband in the Louvre's cafe
to sip the steaming tea and chew on his poetry,
we're off like schoolgirls, screeching in duet,
dazzled by the bright eternal gasp of ancient things.

We've got no business here, homegirl and compañera,
we've got no business working our mouths around
this sharp, exquisite language, or savoring the sweet
tongue-squeeze of pastries, glossy cakes and shaved chocolate.

We're of simpler stock—city and country dust,
collard greens, hopscotch, moonpies, bullet holes
and basement slow dances. We are shamelessly American,
rough street girls with rusty knees, the flip side of cocky
Parisian wisps in slim cashmere coats the color of tobacco.

Girlfriend, you and I are *too* much scream for this place,
but you're a junkie just like I am.

Too long denied access to *official* beauty,
we walk these streets
with our mouths open and faces tilted up,
swallowing everything, swallowing it all,
much too much scenery and sound
for our wee American throats.
We gawk at cathedrals with their gargoyles
bleached to an eerie snarl by bright slashes of moon,
say *goodbye* when we mean *yes,*

good morning when we mean *how much*,
ask for bread when we need the toilet.

We are amazed that no one is asking for all of this back,
that we are allowed to bask in this city's light.

I can still hear my mother,
as plain and practical as a cast-iron skillet—
Chile, you need to stop all that foolishness
over there in some France
where you don't know nothing or nobody!
Ain't no black folks over there no way.

But I know you, old friend,
with your burnished tangle of hair
and deep laugh,
and right now these halls belong to *us*.
There are
bad
girls
loose
in the Louvre,
girls soft as gunshots,
girls nourished and fueled by silvers, silks,
and the stoned gaze of Napoleon.

We laugh at the smashed noses of Egyptian rulers,
stare at the tiny mummified feet of a young girl,
mistake Goya for Gauguin
and rub what surfaces we can,
including the marble cocks of towering deities.
When we say things like,
Hey, I think I saw this one on a postcard once!
or, *Do you know*

how old
this thing is?
how can the world help but love us?
We would give Venus *our* arms.

After seven hours
clicking our hungry heels
and snapping illicit flash photos
in dark halls brimming with whispered music,
we finally find the *Mona Lisa,*
alone,
caged and antiseptic
behind that glass every woman wears.
And we wonder how best to free her,
knowing she's a junkie just like we are.

She longs for our wild voices,
our naive, accidental beauty.
She's achin' to ditch that frame
and skip these hallowed halls with the homegirls,
mistake the obscene for the exquisite,
and gaze at unsolved mysteries
that just for once
are not her own.

Biting Back

Children do not grow up
as much as they grow away.
My son's eyes are stones—flat, brown, fireless,
with no visible openings in or out.
His voice, when he cares to try it on,
hovers one-note in that killing place
where even the blues fidget.
Tight syllables, half-spoken, half-spat,
greet me with the warmth
of glint-tipped arrows. The air around him
hurts my chest, grows too cold to nourish,
and he stares past me to the open door of his room,
anxious for my patented stumbling retreat.

My fingers used to brush bits of the world
from his kinked hair,
but he has moved beyond that mother shine
to whispered *fucks* on the telephone,
to the sweet mystery of pearl buttons
dotting the maps of young girls,
to the warped, frustrating truths of algebra,
to anything
but me.
Ancient, annoying apparatus,
I have somehow retained the ability
to warm meat,
to open cans,
to clean clothing
that has yellowed and stiffened.
I spit money when squeezed,
don't try to dance in front of his friends,
and know that rap music cannot be stopped.

For these brief flashes of cool, I am tolerated
in spurts.

At night, I lie in my husband's arms
and he tells me that these are things that happen,
that the world will tilt right again
and my son will return,
unannounced,
as he was—
goofy and clinging, clever with words, stupefied by rockets.
And I dream on that.

One summer after camp,
twelve inches taller than the summer before,
my child grinned and said,
Maybe a tree bit me.

We laughed,
not knowing that was to be his last uttered innocence.
Only months later, eyes narrowed and doors slammed.
Now he is scowls, facial hair, knots of muscle.
He is man smell, grimy fingers, red eyes, rolling dice.
He is street, smoke, cocked cannon.

I sit on his bare mattress after he's left for school,
wondering at the jumble of this motherless world,
look for clues that some gumpopping teenage girl
now wears my face. Full of breast milk and finger songs,
I stumble the street staring at other children,
gulping my dose of their giggles,
and cursing the trees
for their teeth.

The Architect

For Little Richard

I am the architect of rock and roll!
I said I am the—wait a minute, is this mic on—I said
I'm the architect of rock and roll! Now that Elvis,
he was a pretty boy, he sure could sing,
and Lord knows he sho nuff dead now y'all,
but he wouldn't have been him
if it wasn't for me.
I took long sounds like *eeee* and *oooo* and *ahhh*
and had them white kids rubbing up 'gainst each other
making them sparks
that made them fires
their mamas and daddies couldn't *put* out.
Now that Jerry Lee Lewis—shame on that boy
marrying that baby and calling it love—now I might
surrender to a little peach makeup now and then
and outline these big eyes in black,
but I ain't into sinning with no babies. Yeah, I'm hip
to what he could do with a piano,
make those keys rise up and dance on their own,
but you couldn't call what come out of that boy's throat singing,
you'd think somebody was choking that boy!
Now the key to it—
you know, did I tell you, wait a minute now,
did I tell you *I'm* the architect of rock and roll?
Now the key to it is the squeal, my eyes wide open
and gleaming like a crazy colored boy, white folks
see that one time and it *scares* 'em—they trip all over
each other running out to buy the record.

Now I ain't never been what you'd call *sexy*,
at least not in the normal way,
but I been burning the kinks outta this hair ever since I could,
and I can still turn the eyes
of some young boy
aching to hook on to a legend.
If I do say so *my*self,
I still got my hips,
still got that smooth line
straight down to the point in my patent leathers,
still turn some eyes now and then.

But when I'm up onstage
I sit my pretty ass right down behind that piano.
Chuck Berry, that ol' fool, kicking and duckwalking,
he know he too old for that teenage mess,
and makin' them dirty movies on the side.
You know, I'm 'bout the only one who stayed pure,
partial as I am to a little eyeliner now and then,
I done kept clean.

Ain't fathered but two babies in this life—
named one Rock and the other one Roll—
that's them in your ear.

Now you can call me sissy,
but I'm the builder,
I'm the breath,
I'm the man you wants to pretend you was.
Bee bop a loo bop a bop bam boom, baby,
I'm the architect—
and the building ain't finished yet.

Skinhead

They call me skinhead. And I got my own beauty.
It is knife-scrawled across my back in sore, jagged letters,
it's in the way my eyes snap away from the obvious.
I sit in my dim matchbox, on the edge of a bed tousled
with my ragged smell,
slide razors across my hair,
count how many ways
I can bring blood closer to the surface of my skin.
These are the duties of the righteous,
the ways of the anointed.

The face that moves in my mirror is huge and pockmarked,
apple-cheeked, scraped pink and brilliant,
I am filled with my own spit.
Two years ago, a machine that slices leather
sucked in my hand and held it,
whacking off three fingers at the root.
I didn't feel nothing till I looked down
and saw one of them on the floor
next to my boot heel,
and I ain't worked since then.

I sit here and watch niggers take over my TV set,
walking like kings up and down the sidewalks in my head,
walking like their fat black mamas *named* them freedom.
Well, my shoulders tell me that ain't right.

So I move out into the sun
where my beauty makes them lower their heads,
or into the night
with a lead pipe up my sleeve,
a razor in my boot.
I was born to make things right.

It's easy now to move my big body into shadows,
to move from a place where there was nothing
into the stark circle of a streetlight,
the pipe raised up high over my head.
It's a kick to watch their eyes get big,
round and gleaming like cartoon jungle boys,
right in that second they know the pipe's gonna
come down, and I got this I like to say, listen,
I say *Hey, nigger, Abe Lincoln's been dead a long time!*

I get hard listening to their skin burst.
I was born to make things right.

Then this newspaper guy comes around,
seems I was a little sloppy kicking some fag's ass
and he opened up his hole and screamed about it.
So this reporter finds me at home in my bed,
TV flashes licking my face clean.
Same ol' shit.
Ain't got no job,
the coloreds and spics got 'em.
Why ain't I working? Look at my *hand*, asshole.
No, I not part of no organized group,
I'm just a white boy who loves his race,
fighting for a pure country.
Sometimes it's just me,
sometimes three,
sometimes 30.
AIDS will take care of the faggots,
then it's gonna be white on black in the streets.
Then there'll be three *million*.
I tell him that.

So he writes it up
and I come off looking like I'm some kinda goddamned freak,
like I'm Hitler himself. I ain't that lucky,
but I got my own beauty.
It's in my steel-toed boots,
in the hard corners of my shaved head.

I look in the mirror and hold up my mangled hand,
only the baby finger left,
I know its the wrong goddamned finger,
but *fuck you all anyway.*
I'm riding the top rung of the perfect race,
my face scraped pink and brilliant.
I'm your baby, America, your boy,
Drunk on my own spit, I am goddamned fuckin' beautiful.

And I was born
and raised
right here.

In the Ultimate Blues Bar

men sip their bitter cocktails,
slide damp dollars across the bar,
and wheeze in rhythm,
resenting the relentless thump
of their late-night hearts.
They speak fondly of natural disasters,
predict how the missing child
will be found naked beneath a blanket of dead leaves.

Someone pops a quarter in the jukebox,
and feet tap to the dirge of downbeats,
the been-done-wrong grunts
that slug through the blood like a blind fighter.

When a woman rips a man open,
this is where he comes to bleed.

I shoulda known the bitch was no good!
screams a truck driver from his corner table,
I shoulda seent she was what she was.
The circus lights from the jukebox
break across his face,
fill his toothless mouth with color
as he screams the name *Janet!*,
as he curses it up and down the greasy walls,
drags it in the muck on the floor in front of his friends.
He pulls the name back up on the table
and he tries to slice his wrists with it,
he holds the name up against his skull
and waits for it to scatter his brains,
he swallows it
and sits death still
so the poison can creep into his blood.

He takes the name *Janet!*
and he rocks the room with it,
I shoulda seent she was no good for me,
I shoulda listened to my friends,
I shoulda looked deep into her smoky black eyes
and walked out on what they told me,
and and dammit dammit—
Janet!
and screaming the name over and over
like he's purging his belly of bad whiskey,
he staggers to the jukebox and plays
another long slow song
by a blind black man.

Tonight he's got that run from Moline to Macon,
and Janet will sleep curled in a bigger bed,
a deep purple gash over her eye,
another man on her mind.

Bless them.
Bless them as they weep on their own sagging shoulders,
rolling the soft syllables of love around in their mouths.

Bless them
as they fill the bartender's ear
with blues she pretends she's never heard,
as she nods patiently to every twist of their gut,
bless them
as even the shot glasses
take on the curves of women.

Bless them
as the barkeep closes shop
and our boys link wobbly arms

and croon their blues to an amused moon
who bends their hearts
until she realizes
that only a woman
has the balls
to break them.

Olive Oyl Talks to *People* Magazine

If you must know me, first know this—
I was born a bone child,
a bleached confusion of sticks
clattering from my mother's womb,
ribs fused gently around a sputtering heart.
No milk moved in the woman who made me,
so I lay in her rangy arms
sucking the thought of the sea from her skin.

My father was a stevedore,
wrists of dust, his skinny pink neck
bulging with pull and push, heft and release.
My mother grew weak trying to love him,
searching for the rhythms of water
in the way his sour body folded around sleep,
his brusque demands for sex, more potatoes.
She sat at the window, watching *real* sailors.

He blossomed as her body cramped with me—
he was praying for a boy, muscles he could tame,
a fool who'd believe he was seaworthy.
But then I came—blanched, sickly,
slick with blood and effort,
hair as black and flat as a seal's.
He never held me,
and only touched me once,

his fingers tangling
in my sparse pubic hair,
then pulling away,
startled, disgusted, thrilled.
He went no further
because he only *called* himself a sailor.

Early one morning as he helped a crew
unload the *Windswept*, his heart splintered
and burst, his body falling only inches from
the sea he'd sworn to possess before he died.
His mouth filled with earth and chips of wood.
My mother screamed, refused food, followed.

I was left alone in the house of my birth,
a battered wooden shell ravaged by wind and salt.
My wide eyes were trained on the water line,
watching the rickety ships bob and pivot, hearing
the raw shouts, the thick voices of mariners.

I was still a stick interrupted by knees,
ending in huge feet caged in black shoes.
I pulled my hair tight and looped a red ribbon
through the floppy bun, powdered coy circles
on drained cheeks, stuffed napkins into the front
of my dress and pranced the shore, a sacrifice
of sticks. I wanted the man my father had wanted
to be, a man of the sea, drunk with horizons.
But the rumbling one came first.

He was all sinew and teeth, arms like tree trunks,
muscles squalling inside stiff cotton clothing.
I never knew a real name. The men barked, *Bluto!*
and the hard syllables swirled in my head.
A look from him would have folded my father,
made my mother press her face against the window.
The helpless air crackled when he was in it,
sparks stung my skin, currents bristled my hair.
Love made me dance around him, silly with want,
my hard black brogans clicking on the dock.
My wretched waltz amused and confused him,

until he had no way to imagine the night without me.
Ribs tightened hard around my sputtering heart.

No woo music or slow fingers. He took me like
a windstorm, left me rattled and chafed. His brash
laughter boomed, and a curious crowd gathered
at my window to watch him suck tiny red stars into
the skin of my throat. He took me against the wall,
pinned to the splintered floor, in the chipped porcelain
tub, against the icebox, from the front, from behind,
with his mouth and with a cock veined as a horse's neck.
I wept with romance, bled into his cupped hand.

Whenever he sailed, I followed, walking the world's
water in my hard shoes. He passed me to his drooling
men, roped me to the bow, guffawed at my longing.
On faraway islands bursting with color I could smell,
he starved me,
tied me to tree trunks,
teased my body with ravenous tigers.
Each night he rewarded my devotion,
biting into my skin with yellowed teeth,
another letter of his gruff name
carved into my want. I only wanted him
to love me more than water.

But one raucous midnight, while I prayed no train
would come rumbling down the tracks I was tied
to, the ropes loosened and I was swept into arms
I didn't know. I looked up into a comical squint,
smelled the briny musk of his panting,
and wondered what seas this man had seen.

If Bluto was tidal wave, Popeye was ripple.
Bald, nearly blind, bubble-cheeked, a rotting pipe
teetering on his bottom lip—
my savior.
As if I had asked to be saved.
I hated him, his giddy, toothless smile,
that stupid giggle, his bulging cartoon forearms.

When he saw my scars, he blubbered like a baby,
weeping at my histories of torn skin,
not recognizing the signposts of love.
I fell asleep counting, while his mouth
touched each one.

I had no place for him in my crazy life,
yet there he was.
When he loved me,
laying me down as if I were a rose,
my wounds found new skin.
I was too beautiful to be me.

But now my life borders on slapstick.
I walk into traps, tumble into rushing rivers.
Bluto dangles me over spitting volcanoes,
snatches me from Popeye's bed, slams his want
into me, threatens me with blades.
Popeye gobbles something green and risks
his life to find me, beats Bluto senseless,
then it all begins again.
My rawboned body stretches between them,
threatens to snap.

Popeye wants to marry me, make an honest
woman out of a hot, bony stevedore's daughter.
Bluto lights a match, teases my scarred nipple.

You ask how I can want them both,
how these bones have carried them for so long.
If you must know, first know this—
I was raised by the water,
crafted by these tides,
a stick child, never wise or beautiful.
Whatever I loved loved the water first.
And I will die possessing these sailing men
who fight over my frail body,
craving this flesh,
and neglecting the sea.

Chinese Cucumbers

it's 3 pm on one helluva hot day and he'd been
scouring the close cluttered streets nonstop,
forgetting lunch. it's 3 pm exactly one week
after a headline screeched and screamed at him
from a checkout rag, CHINESE CUCUMBERS
MIRACLE CURE FOR AIDS and in the middle
of poking around another cobwebbed stall,
slapping aside the maggots and woozy fruit flies,
he realizes he doesn't know what the damn things
look like. and once he found them, if he ever did,
what next? should he peel them, mash them, dice
them, boil them, sauté them, or simply roll them
across the angry blotches on David's skin? should
he share them with David, folding shards into his
lover's mouth, send one to each of their useless
friends, pray over them, torch them as sacrifice
or simply swirl them into a ridiculous casserole?
maybe the cure was just in the finding—maybe
as soon as a babbling backdoor merchant found
the last batch ever stashed in a storeroom, David
would spring up in his hospital bed, wide-eyed,
to say *hey where'd all this breath come from*, yes,
that was what David would say and how he would
say it. maybe the damn things weren't deliverance
after all, maybe they were just like the oil, that
clouded bottle of pepperminty funk it took a year
to find, and when he did he warmed a thousand
plump drops between his palms and rubbed
them over David's balls, the withering cock, up
and down his scrawny legs, between his toes. then
he turned the shell of his man over and massaged
David's ass and back and waited and waited and

waited and waited but the oil just glowed loud
and slick under the lamplight, and David just kept
on dying, dying so loud he had to cover his ears
against it, but sound seeped through NEW CURE
ON THE HORIZON, crystals—yes, crystals, just
hang one from his neck on a solid gold chain, make
sure it's set at just the right angle, Oprah,
Phil, *Nightline, Current Affair* so it simply has to be
true, and he cradled David's head in his lap, slipped
the chain down on toothpick neck, a purply crystal
burning with a wrong light, glittery as fuck against
David's breastbone, shaking with his half-breaths
and not working not working not working but ugly
pretty and loud as shit *I am one gorgeous chunk*
of glass but what is inside this body I cannot pull
out, I cannot shush the clicking and wheezing or
purify the lumps of blood, but listen, have you tried

the oils?

made a near-dead boy in the south end get up outta
his bed and scream hallelujah! but somewhere he
read that that greased-up boy was also on something
called the spiritual path repeating one thousand times
a day *i am a good person, my body is pure, i will not*
die, i am a good person, my body is pure, i will not die,
and as he guides David through words hurting in his
mouth, oil matting his hair, a sapped crystal waning
on his chest (*he is a good person, his body is pure,*
please don't let him die) and tomorrow wouldn't be
nearly so hot, he'd search all damn day if he had to
and CHINESE CUCUMBERS MIRACLE CURE
FOR AIDS and Jesus Christ, the damn things had to be
somewhere

Close to Death, 1993

That's her boy on the cover. All feral and clueless and when she tells him to try hard to look like the name of the book he doesn't change his face at all. She reads "Undertaker" at a public housing meeting and a woman runs out of the room because she sees her own gone boy on the slab being sliced and sewn and rebirthed for viewing. What's the difference, the poet thinks, between a sonnet and a limerick and a pantoum and all those rooms poets build for lines to live in? Poems are really for people who don't read them—the barber who babbles an endless stream of gleeful shit, the preacher who moonwalks the pulpit, the undertaker who can't meet the eyes of a young mother. They're for her son and all the sons and brothers and fathers who keep moving closer and closer and closer and their faces don't change at all.

Edward or Edwin
Outside Boston City Hospital

Despite his sour smell, tangled snaps of hair,
wiry knotted beard, he looks fine. Yet he hovers
outside Emergency as if he were waiting
to be scooped up on a gurney and ushered inside.
My name is Edward. Spies a reporter's notebook,
changes his mind: *Edwin. I'm not sick.*

What the old folks used to call blue black, Edward
sweats under three layers of prickly, matted clothing,
the top shell mostly wool. It is a July hungry for casualties.
Tattered duffle sports the worn words "Parker's Garage."
From time to time, he raises an empty plastic milk container
to his left eye, peers inside. Shakes it, looks again.
I got a home. Ain't homeless.

A young girl, unraveled braids and laces,
tucks a baby boy away like a football,
uses her free hand to smack the one who drags behind—
saucer-eyed, sniffling, not much older than three.
I done told you to shut up, boy, didn't I? she hisses,
her eyes glazed and tired, her voice a child's voice.
That's why I don't never want to take you no place.
I'm gon' kill you if you don't be quiet.
Edwin's red eyes widen.
Leave that boy alone, he growls,
not loud enough for the girl to hear.
Nuff killin' going on round here.
Ain't nothing but a baby yourself.

Clutching his duffle, he backs up a few steps,
dizzied by sun singing on glass and metal.

Through the windows, there is much scurrying.
Got a brother dying in there, Edward says.
Died two years ago.
Cancer eating up his blood,
took him on 'way from here.

Inside the hospital, workers and equipment move so fast
they leave behind paintbrush strokes of white and silver.
Edwin is afraid of the sick, afraid of discovering
that he is sick himself, afraid of a dark biting in his blood.
Another young girl walks by
with another baby trembling in his blanket.
Important white men jostle the mother
as they pass. Anthony Jamal Crayton
has been shaking for two days.

Two women sit and chatter.
They are cool, polished, obviously late for work.
One munches from a bag of chips,
the other looks up now and again from a tattered paperback.
Ain't nothing wrong with Michael, he just acting.
The taller woman's nails are red, squared.
Just want somebody to be feeling sorry for him.
Ain't nothing wrong with his heart 'cept I done broke
it too many times. Edwin hears a blues lyric, would
growl it crass and keyless if he could. He is still

on the sidewalk, stuffing something into his duffle,
glaring at the busted zipper.
Even in the jalapeno heat, he balances
all of his home on his back,
mumbles something about going to see his brother,
peeks once again at the mysteries of the milk carton.

Edward is not sure how old he is.
Old enough to know better, he snorts.
Asked how long he has lived in Boston,
Edwin cackles,
displaying front teeth as black as he is.
He laughs as a fly struggles in his hair.
Girl, you's a fool. This ain't Boston. We in St. Louis.

And inside Boston City Hospital
the beds sag with dying black men,
their minds gone,
their bodies shocked by the heart's treachery,
their whole lives filling their chests.
And Edward won't ever go inside,
afraid of the men that wear his brother's face,
his father's face,
then his.

Terrell's Take on Things

Well, look who come walkin' into my barbershop,
still wearing that Jheri curl. Man, it's almost 2000,
and ain't nobody got no time for grease trickling
all down they neck, 'specially hot as it is out there.
C'mere, lemme clip that shit down. Let them naps
grow out. Couple o' weeks, I'll hook you up with
a fade. Sisters don't like putting they hands in that
greasy mess and did y'all see that chile 'Retha
onstage at the President's thang, trailing all that
fur like she Queen Lizabeth, all that fat unnerneath
it? Ain't never seen no black woman with money
stay fat. Chicken see her coming even the *bones*
get scared. That chile will eat a spaghetti *strap*.
What that song she sang, *Ain't No Way*? Well, I
guess it sho' ain't. She got one chance, tho. Stay
alive long enough, *time* make you skinny. I just
don't know if she got that much time. Wait, look
out the window, there go that gal I was telling
y'all 'bout, Lawd, got enough ass to set a drink on.
I'm gon' be knee deep in that come Saturday night
or my name ain't Terrell Anderson Jr. and I ain't
got my hands tusslin' in y'all nappy heads. Man,
she don't know me yet, but she will. I bet she done
already heard 'bout how my lovemaking done put
a few sisters on crutches, how I done whipped
some o' this nature on them, now they drooling,
barking like hound dogs. Hell, y'all can laugh if
y'all want. Thomas, ask your sister. And you over
there laughing, ask yo mama. They say size don't
matter, but it do if it's *this* size, man, I have to bind
this shit to my leg or it would scare all y'all up
outta here. Come Saturday night, you can ask that
gal y'all just seen. She be passing by that window

in a wheelchair. Mark my words. And Thomas,
speaking of women, one too many times I done
seen your wife over there cross the street up in
that butcher shop, and the meat she asking for ain't
what makes it to your table for supper. Man, she
in there all day, going all behind the counter like she
all of a sudden interested in the butcher business.
What she interested in is the butcher's *business* and
you better start asking yourself why. You better start
taking care of stuff at your own home, my man, 'fore
she get a taste of that sausage he selling, then you be
up in here crying 'bout *she gone, she gone.* Man, you
can't be climbing up on top of no woman like you
got somewhere else to be in five minutes. And there
you is, up in the Continental every Friday, sniffing
all up Deborah Ann's pretty young butt like she want
something from you besides that money you always
waving around. Man, anytime you see flies buzzing
around a woman—and it ain't summer—it's time
to move on to another woman. Damn, your wife got
some nice legs on her, too, if that butcher don't take
her up on it, I might get in line. Charlie, what about
your boy? Damned near 40, no woman in sight.
Could be he just ugly, though. Other night I heard
a *blind* woman turning him down, said she could just
imagine how ugly he was. And Ed, what you talking
'bout "Put in some curl," talking 'bout some activator,
you better activate your head up under this razor
and lemme cut that shit outta there. This the 1990s,
man. *Black. man. free. now.* Superfly done flew.
Been doing this 40 years. This is Terrell's Afrocentric
Barbershop Fade Palace and Wild Style Emporium.
Now put you ass in that chair,
and put your head
in my hands.

Daddy Braids My Hair 1962

At first he rhythmed on the crown of a dust mop,
threading the tattered gray ropes under, over, through,
then under again, breaking into an uneven man beat,
weaving a thick tube that slithered loose whenever
his hands rested. I watched from our one good kitchen chair,
Sears Best gone bad, my freshly Prelled hair
as tangled as gossip and dry as straw,
a jar of sweet warm oil balanced in my lap,
a comb strong for the taming of mannish hair
wedged in my kinks, poised for that first tug.

But my father, who'd volunteered so eagerly for duty
that morning, first had to practice on the dusty
unprotesting head of a mop. I stared as he looped
the precise length over and over, sometimes lifting
his eyes to stare at the explosion atop my head,
clearly preferring the mop's droopy Caucasian strands,
its absence of mouth. By the time he was ready for me,
the fragrant hair oil had begun to cool.

He pried the comb from the explosion and his hands
hovered there for an uncertain moment. Thin fist gathered
what it could, then the whining drag of the comb, popping each
nap with baby bullet sounds. Tears filled my shoulders,
made me shake. While working the oil through, he kicked in
with a low note. He was singing. How could he sing?
I didn't believe he was singing. *If you ever* ouch, daddy,
don't pull so hard *change your mind* really daddy, put some
more grease on it don't pull so hard *about leaving,*
leaving me behind you know what mama does daddy?
She presses it. She uses a comb hot off the fire that makes it easier
oh oh bring it to me he's singing he's singing and my

scalp's burning up *bring your sweat lovin'* he's calling
back the mop beat, under, through, then under again,
but pulling now, pulling *bring it all home to me* ouch *yeah*
ouch *yeah* ouch *yeah*, and I will never forget
his smile, warm as butter on cornbread, as he inspected handiwork.
So what if the part was jagged, braids all different lengths
of too greasy hair unraveling? We're off for ice cream,
all twin bowlegs and bravado and holding hands,
me showing off my shiny head to snickering Deborah Johnson,
my daddy with another low song growing in his throat.

The Room with the Star

For Little Richard

The architect of rock and roll sashays offstage,
pokes his weary veneer with a pearl-tipped hat pin
and grits his perfect teeth. The celebrated attitude
hisses from his skin, angry air from a pinched balloon.
He is left aching, cramped, nearly folded,
doubtful that the ringing cheers can spark revival,
and he waits for some hopeful, babyfaced boy diva
to take his hand, guide him past dusty backdrops
to his door, the one with the silver star.

The damned room is all light. Fat glaring bulbs
line the mirrored walls, the mirrored doors,
snicker beneath fringed shades. Lights sway from
the mirrored ceiling, dot the lazily circling 4-blade fan.
Even with his eyes shut, he is everywhere,
blotched beige in the snarling illumination,
the slick inflated pompadour glistening an overload
of oil, eyes black double-outlined and wounded.
There are too many of his mouths,
stained as a debutante's,
born to pout that pretty, thank you, never was
no question. This is always where the dizzy comes,
in these rooms where he cannot turn
without more of him being there, hundreds of bellies
girdled to flatness beneath rhinestone buttons,
thousands of wounded legs, still hiccuping with backbeat.

He'd been a god, his hair dripping venom,
Jesus, he'd played the piano with his knees, his feet,
even one kickass riff from his store-bought teeth.
He bit into microphones, chewed, crazy but helpless,

spat lyric at the jealous whores in the front row,
what he did was lose his natural mind. He took 'em
to church again, holy-rolled them till their backs cracked.
He saw it begin with the white boys loosening their ties.
It always hit them first, the ones who cackled when they
first saw the heaven-bound arch of Vaselined brows
and that prized Georgia peach complexion,
the ones who just couldn't believe they'd plunked down
20 bucks a seat because their girlfriends wanted to see
some dusty colored queen. So he shot it into their bones,
compromised their religion with it, threatened their spines
with devil. Lawd, he made them boogie with their cocks in the air.
"That old black faggot got you in his spell …
that old black faggot thought you knew so well—"

And he got their girls too. Bent those pale little bodies back
and got that moan working right in there
where it shoulda been, leaving honey-colored starfish streaks
in the crotch of all those pink Republican panties.
Rock done truly rolled here tonight!
Got to that point where the walls bulged with gospel,
where a room full of disciples would have sold their souls
if he'd wailed the request.
Now put *that* on a stamp. Build a shrine to *that* in Memphis.

They wanted a bitch? They got one. He worked the room,
screamed at the screamers to scream and when they
screamed, he screamed at them to shut the fuck up.
He trilled, pranced, rolled his eyes back into his head.
Damn right, he was possessed. *Built ALL this shit,* he told them.
Designed it, named it, pushed it out from between MY legs.

Went for two hours tonight, but Lord, paying for it now,
out of the spotlight, moving like an old man, an old man,

an old man, an old man, all these mirrors. Time to begin
the slow peel, glittered raiment unbuttoned, unzippered,
unsnapped, and falling. Time to free the soft belly from its
spandex cage, to ease off pointed, patent kickers.
Time, in secret, to be unpretty. Fistfuls of tissue streak
with the peachy color of white women,
of bravely swaying boys, of that bitch Nancy Wilson.
He scrapes the eyeliner off with his pointer finger, curses
as the black wax cakes beneath this morning's perfect manicure.
He turns blacker, smaller. In the center of the lit repeating,
weariness crooks his back and he eases himself to
the lush carpet, lying cool and broken on a pile of loud clothing.
That infernal Muzak slithers in. He is naked a million times.

Undertaker

For Floyd Williams

When a bullet enters the brain, the head explodes.
I can think of no softer warning for the mothers
who sit doubled before my desk,
knotting their smooth brown hands,
and begging, *fix my boy, fix my boy.*
Here's his high school picture.
And the smirking, mildly mustachioed player
in the crinkled snapshot
looks nothing like the plastic bag of boy
stored and dated in the cold room downstairs.
In the picture, he is cocky and chiseled,
clutching the world by the balls. I know the look.
Now he is flaps of cheek,
slivers of jawbone, a surprised eye,
assorted teeth, bloody tufts of napped hair.
The building blocks of my business.

I swallow hard, turn the photo facedown
and talk numbers instead. The high price
of miracles startles the still-young woman,
but she is prepared. I know that she has sold
everything she owns, that cousins and uncles
have emptied their empty bank accounts,
that she dreams of her baby
in tuxedoed satin, flawless in an open casket,
a cross or blood-red rose tacked to his fingers,
his halo set at a cocky angle.
I write a figure on a piece of paper
and push it across to her
while her chest heaves with hoping.
She stares at the number, pulls in

a slow weepy breath: *Jesus.*
But Jesus isn't on my payroll. I work alone
until the dim insistence of morning,
bent over my grisly puzzle pieces, gluing,
stitching, creating a chin with a brushstroke.
I plop glass eyes into rigid sockets,
then carve eyelids from a forearm, an inner thigh.
I plump shattered skulls, and paint the skin
to suggest warmth, an impending breath.
I reach into collapsed cavities to rescue
a tongue, an ear.
Lips are never easy to re-create.

And I try not to remember the stories,
the tales the mothers must tell me
to ease their own hearts. *Oh,* they cry,
my Ronnie, my Willie, my Michael, my Chico.
It was self-defense. He was on his way home,
a dark car slowed down, they must have thought
he was someone else. He stepped between
two gang members at a party.
Really, he was trying to get off the streets,
he was trying to pull away from the crowd.
He was in the wrong place at the wrong time.
Fix my boy. He was a good boy. Make him the way he was.

But I have explored the jagged gaps
in the boy's body, I have smoothed the angry edges
of bullet holes. I have touched him in places
no mother knows, and I have birthed his new face.
I know he believed himself invincible,
that he most likely hissed *Fuck you, man!* before the bullets
lifted him off his feet. I try not to imagine
his swagger, his lizard-lidded gaze,
his young mother screaming into the phone.

She says she will find the money, and I know
this is the truth that fuels her, forces her
to place one foot in front of the other.

I want to take her down to the chilly room, open the bag
and shake its terrible bounty onto the magic steel table.
I want her to see him,
to touch him,
to press her lips to the frozen flap of cheek.
The woman needs to wither,
finally,
and move on.

We both jump as the phone rattles in its hook.
I pray it's my wife, a bill collector, a wrong number.
But the wide, questioning silence on the other end
is too familiar.
Another mother needing a miracle.
Another homeboy coming home.

A Poem for the Man Who Shot My Father

I don't know where you are now,
so for the purposes of this poem
I will imagine you dead.
The circumstances of your death
should be ironic. A bullet smashes into
the back of your skull. A bullet
smashes into the back
of your skull. A bullet smashes
into the back
of your skull.

A coincidence.

For the purposes of this poem, but only
for the purposes
of this poem,
I will imagine you in a hell
where you are scraped and torched
each second, every second,
and you feel it all,
you feel everything.

For the purposes of this poem
I would like you to describe
my father's face
the moment he turned
and saw you
        wild-eyed and thirsty
the moment he knew
the moment before he turned away
to run

And for the purposes
of this poem, I hold
that picture in my head. I will live
over

and
over
that look of an animal dazed
in the headlights

because, even though
I have imagined you dead,
you are probably not too dead to remember
that there is a hell
here too.

The Dark Magicians

1993, and questions about another suicide
in a Mississippi jail. Southern trees
still dragged down by weight long relieved
and ashy brothers full of remembering
hiss old Delta lyrics, building spittle
on their chins. We are the river wall,
they whisper, the odd lump in a summered soil.
We are the disappeared, desolate and misplaced,
dark magicians stronger than any root or conjure.
Knotting the weathered noose, we slip it down
to circle our throats, pull it to choking and jump,
our hands tied behind our backs the whole time.

In His Room. With Him Gone.

She walks into her son's room without knocking,
more a voyeur than a nurturer,
and is knocked back
by the rancid air
that says *man*.
Again she is surrounded by the remnants
of a life lived desperately—
seven baseball caps sporting the insignia of the moment,
crumpled fast food bags,
foil packets ripped of their rubbers,
posters of snarling rappers with guns in their hands
and ice in their names. She can still smell
her son, the deep musky growl of him,
even though he is miles away,
anxious, shackled. The phone rings,
and it is another child with a mustache
and a roar in his throat. She pictures him
on all fours, snarling, the receiver in his teeth,
sniffing the air for her son's blood.

Spinning 'Til You Get Dizzy

For Dizzy Gillespie

It was never control we were after.
Jazz, by ragged definition, pump-started
its own heart, sensed the potential of chaos
long before it became brown baby lullaby,
the ripples that pulse on the surface of whiskey.

Jazz demanded the unbridling of so many souls,
turned order into impetuous melody—
chords which spewed spit at their captors,
and there was nowhere to run and even
fewer places to hide.

What gave birth to jazz—what moist
constricted passage it struggled from, who held
it aloft, slapped that newborn ass
and sparked the glorious squalling—
doesn't matter. What matters is fluid

line shredding into scat and us
owning that sweetness. What matters
is cigarette-thin men scowling
at their reflections in the bartop. What matters
is sugar browns hitching up homemade skirts
and pounding holes into the dance floor, out past
curfew and tired of asking the time.
What matters is the bee in the bonnet of bebop,
curses swirling from the mouth of a sax, moans
trapped in a cool column of clarinet, the blues twisting
a guitar's stringed throat, and mojo rising up
from the brown battered skin of drums.

There is growling in all of this,
a warning to stop and shout *hallelujah!*
from wherever you are, to shout praise
for all that is chill and raunchy, to be thankful
for complication.
And let somebody else answer
when the disbelieving ask *Who is jazz's mama?*
What ripe woman's body curved and struggled
and pushed that hardheaded boy into the light?

And somewhere, the bell of a horn curved up.
Because, you see, it was never about control,
it was never about polished brass eking out strained notes
for maybe brown babies in sequins and hardbacked chairs.
Jazz was never capture or compliance,
it was all about the possibilities of chaos, and he
never bothered straightening that bell,
'cause why shouldn't heaven get the gospel too?

What he blew upset us, soured our gentle stomachs.
What did we need with music that thrived in blue light,
music with rumbling in its feet?
We begged it to go away, banned it on the airwaves,
'cause the heat in our hips spoke otherwise.
Couldn't do, wouldn't do, didn't know how to do without it,
those cocky, seamless blasts that rock us to rolling,
but it was not about control,
it was never about control,
it was about the bell of a horn curved up,
not jazz's mama but her son—
all rough chin and sharkskin,
a black beret on cool kinks,
never a note to apologize for,
and

such

outrageous

cheeks!

A Found Poem

As Far as Blood Goes
is a biographical novel that chronicles
the efforts of a talented, unhappy black youngster
to escape slavery and become a physician
(as is his natural white father).
Though the hero, Michael Mabaya,
is fictional, his accomplishments parallel
those of hundreds of now-forgotten black men and women
who overcame the crushing barriers of their times
to lead lives of quiet achievement and dignity.

Michael Mabaya's story is the stuff of great fiction
for after he achieves his goal and becomes
a respected physician, he draws attention to himself
by reading a controversial paper at a medical convention.

The result:
he is taken back to Virginia to be sold
as a common slave! His only hope
is that his father acknowledges him at last—
and his white brother will come to his rescue!

Reconstruction

For Rodney King

Enough of the horror. Let us consider
the delicate maze of bone in the face,
the eyes glistening and vulnerable,
teeth easily shattered. Let us wonder
at the miracles of patch and knit,
the slick immediacy of scarring,
the swelling that flattens to sinew.
Let's rejoice as human returns to human,
as new tall walking signals rebirth.

Enough of gritty reel. No more
clutching dust, folding against
metronome swing. April already,
another fire simmers. Quick,
let's find the man. Film the mending.

Teahouse of the Almighty, 2006

The poet meets Nicole in a Florida that's too much biting sun, but no sunshine. The little girl's mother had just died of need and needles. Nicole is scrawny and wide-eyed and terrifying when she asks the poet to please undead her mother, *okay?* and *make a poem do that.* The poet takes a deep breath and lies about magic. But it's not really lying, because—

—the teahouse is a real place. The poet drives by it the day she divorces her husband, and wonders and wonders how it feels inside. But it's closed, which gives her permission to see it. The teapot is scarred cast iron, the only tea they serve is murk-gray, peppery and scalding to burn away whatever you want gone. Like a gone mama and grief numbing your little bones. Nicole and the poet have their own table, right by the door. Jesus passes by all the time, trudging and slow-smilin', but He never comes in.

Building Nicole's Mama

For the sixth-grade class of Lillie C. Evans School, Liberty City, Miami

I am astonished at their mouthful names—
Lakinishia, Fumilayo, Chevellanie, Delayo—
their ragged rebellions and lip-glossed pouts,
and all those pants drooped as drapery.
I rejoice when they kiss my face, whisper wet
and urgent in my ear, make me their obsession
because I have brought them poetry.

They shout me raw, bruise my wrists with pulling,
and brashly claim me as mama as they
cradle my head in their little laps,
waiting for new words to grow in my mouth.

You.
You.
You.

Angry, jubilant, weeping poets—we are all
saviors, reluctant hosannas in the limelight,
but you knew that, didn't you? Then let us
bless this sixth-grade class—40 nappy heads,
40 cracking voices, and all of them
raise their hands when I ask. They have all seen
the Reaper, grim in his heavy robe,
pushing the button for the dead project elevator,
begging for a break at the corner pawnshop,
cackling wildly in the back pew of the Baptist church.

I ask the death question and 40 fists
punch the air, *me!, me!* And O'Neal,
matchstick crack child, watched his mother's
body become a claw, and nine-year-old Tiko Jefferson,

barely big enough to lift the gun, fired a bullet
into his own throat after Mama bended his back
with a lead pipe. Tamika cried into a sofa pillow
when Daddy blasted Mama into the north wall
of their cluttered one-room apartment,
Donya's cousin gone in a drive-by. Dark window,
click, click, gone, says Donya, her tiny finger
a barrel, the thumb a hammer. I am shocked
by their losses—and yet when I read a poem
about my own hard-eyed teenager, Jeffery asks

He is dead yet?

It cannot be comprehended,
my 18-year-old still pushing and pulling
his own breath. And those 40 faces pity me,
knowing that I will soon be as they are,
numb to our bloodied histories,
favoring the Reaper with a thumbs-up and a wink,
hearing the question and shouting *me, me,
Miss Smith, I know somebody dead!*

Can poetry hurt us? they ask me before
snuggling inside my words to sleep.

I love you, Nicole says, Nicole wearing my face,
pimples peppering her nose, and she is as black
as angels are. Nicole's braids dipped, their ends
kissed with match flame to seal them,
and *can you teach me to write a poem about my mother?
I mean, you write about your daddy and he dead,
can you teach me to remember my mama?*

A teacher tells me this is the first time Nicole
has admitted that her mother is gone,
murdered by slim silver needles and a stranger
rifling through her blood, the virus pushing
her skeleton through for Nicole to see.
And now this child with rusty knees
and mismatched shoes sees poetry as her scream
and asks me for the words to build her mother again.
Replacing the voice.
Stitching on the lost flesh.

So poets,
as we pick up our pens,
as we flirt and sin and rejoice behind microphones—
remember Nicole.
She knows that we are here now,
and she is an empty vessel waiting to be filled.

And she is waiting.
And she
is
waiting.

And she waits.

Giving Birth to Soldiers

February 1, 2005—Tabitha Bonilla's husband, Army Captain Orlando A. Bonilla, 27, was killed Wednesday in a helicopter accident in Baghdad. Her father, Army Sergeant First Class Henry A. Bacon, 45, died in Iraq last February.

She will pin ponderous medals to her
housedress, dripping the repeated roses,
while she claws through boxes filled with
him and then him. The accepting of God's
weird wisdom takes place over forkfuls
of rubbery casseroles and the snowy vows
of newsmen who measure her worth
in cued weeping. She offers her husband's
hands, a shrine of their mingled smells,
a warm seat on a couch of napped corduroy.
They offer one polished bone, scrubbed
clean of war. And she babbles of links and
irony, shrugs her numb shoulders, and feels
dimly blessed as a door slams shut on both
sides of her head. Suddenly, she is her
only history. Smiling politely beneath a fierce
salute, propped upright behind the crumpled
ghosts of her men, she is the catchy logo
for a confounded country. This day is the day
she has. Tomorrow, she will touch her own
breasts, she will dismantle a gaudy altar
with her teeth. And she will ask a bemused God
for guidance as she steps back into line,
her womb tingling vaguely with the next soldier.

The World Won't Wait

On Tuesday, I watched as a 27-year-old man
held an electric toothbrush in his hand.
His fingers fumbled a bit at the switch,
but he flipped it, then sat astounded
as the dry brush shimmied and jumped in his palm.

This run on batteries? he asked,
turning it upside down,
his eyes lit with a toddler's wonder.

Perhaps you see nothing amazing in this.
But let me paint a picture of this man.

His chest is impossibly plumped, thick and rigid,
his skin mapped with stretch marks
where the muscle has exploded beneath.
His shaved head, a field of grizzle and sweet spray,
is peppered with gouges where the blade sensed
his blood and slipped. He is a child of single syllables,
grunts just under the radar:
I need to eat.
I'm real tired.
Think it's gon' rain.
I like that shirt.
He is my
son, crafted of fevers unleashed and jailhouse iron.
And now, with the clear beyond cry, I see
that his punishment was never there,
among the scabbed tattoos, sluggish clocks, open toilets.
His sentence began in the free, in that moment
when he turned a cheap chugging red toothbrush
over and over in his huge hands and said,
Look at this, Ma. Wow, look at this.

Listening at the Door

Beneath the door, I could practically see
the wretched slither of tobacco and English Leather.
Hiding on the other side, I heard Mama giggle
through clenched teeth, which meant potential
husband sitting spitshined on our corduroy couch.
The needle hit that first groove and I wondered
why my mama had chosen the blues,
wrong, Friday-angled, when it was hope
she needed. I pressed my ear against the door,
heard dual damp panting, the Murphy bed squeal,
the occasional directive,
the sexless clink of jelly jar glasses.

What drove me to listen on those nights
when my mother let that fragrant man in,
banished me to the back of the apartment,
pretended she could shine above hurting?
I'd rest my ear against the cool wood all night
as she flipped through the 45s—
looking for Ray Charles, Stevie Wonder,
somebody blind this time,
somebody crawling on his knees toward love.

My Million Fathers, Still Here Past

Hallelujah for grizzled lip, snuff chew, bended slow walk,
and shit talkin'. Praise fatback, pork gravy, orange butter,
Alaga syrup, grits, and egg sammiches on Wonder Bread
slathered with Hellmann's, mashed 'tween sheets of wax
paper. You hoard that food like money. You are three-day
checker games, pomade slick back, deep brown drink
sucked through holes where teeth once was. You're that
can't-shake lyric, that last bar stool before the back door.

All glory to the church deacons, bodies afloat in pressed
serge, nappy knobs of gray hair greased flat, close to conk,
cracked tenors teetering and testifying. Bless you postmen
and whip cloth shoeshiners, foremen with burning backs,
porters bowing deep. I hear swear-scowling and gold-tooth
giggling over games of bid whist and craps, then Sunday's
Lucky Struck voices playing call-and-response with
the Good Book's siren song. In the midst of some hymn,
my wilting fathers, I see you young again, you spitshined
and polished, folded at the hips on a sluggish Greyhound,
or colored in the colored car of a silver train chugging past
Pine Bluff, Aliceville, Minneola, Greenwood, Muscle Shoals,
headed north where factories pumped precise gospel
and begged you inside their open mouths. You're the reason

the Saturday moon wouldn't fall. You mail-order zoot suit
wide wing felt hats to dip low over one eye, pimp walkin',
taps hammered into heels, kickin' up hot foot to get down
one time, slow drag blues threading bone and hip bump
when the jukebox teases. All praise to the eagle what flew
on Friday and the Lincoln Mark, the Riviera, the Deuce
and a Quarter, the always too much car for what you were.
You were lucky number, the dream book, the steaming spoon

of black-eyes on day one of every year. Here is to your mojo,
your magic real, roots and conjures and long-dead plants
in cotton pouches. Deftly misled by tiny religions, you spat
on the broom that brushed your foot, stayed left of light poles.

Griots of sloped porch and city walk, you, my million fathers,
still here past chalk outlines, dirty needles, and prison cots,
still here past ass whuppings, tree hangings, and many calls
to war, past J.B. stupor, absent children, and drive-bys.
You survive, scarred and hobbling, choking back dawn ache,
high pressure, dimming and lying eyes, joints that smell thunder.
Here's to the secret of your rotting molars, the tender bump
on your balls, your misaligned back, wild corn on that baby
toe, the many rebellions of your black, tired bodies. I watch
you cluck the hard history of lust past your gums, squeeze
rheumy eyes shut to conjure the dream outline of a woman.

I am a woman.
I will rub your weary head,
dance close to you,
shuck you silver peas for dinner.

He was Otis, my father.
But you are Willie Earl and James and Ernest and Jimmy Lee.
All of you, frail charmers, gentle Delta, bodies curled against
the time gone, the time coming. I grieve you tottering toward
death, I celebrate you clinging to life. Open bony dark-veined
arms and receive me, a woman in the shape of your daughter,
who is taking on your last days as her very blood, learning
your whispered language too late to stop your dying,
but not too late
to tell
this story.

How to Be a Lecherous Little Old Black Man and Make Lots of Money

For John Lee Hooker

First, you got to get the blues.
This is easy if you are a person of any gender,
and possess a pulse, a cheating lover,
a stalking ex-lover, a used Yugo, a pumping heart,
an empty wallet, a half-dead dog, an empty frigerator,
one last cigarette butt, a good memory, a nosy mama,
a lonely room, a quick trigger, roving eyes,
an addiction to whiskey,
nothing but the clothes on your back,
a jones for your neighbor's wife,
a jones for your wife's neighbor,
a positive test result,
an itching to leave,
an itching to stay,
or any itching where there shouldn't be any.

Rub your hands slow over your body,
feel the valleys, the wrongs. Let misery
chomp your spine toward collapsing,
let it fold your whole self double.
Then you can walk like John Lee Hooker do—
click shuffle, bent over, nose to the ground,
wearing a cocked brim felt fedora that wouldn't dare fall off.
Then you can think like John Lee do—
I'm old as Victrola,
gotta buy a bottle of Mrs. Butterworth's
if I want to feel a woman,
but I can still

sing better

than you

Map Rappin'

For John Coltrane, and forever for Bruce

I always shudder when I pray.

Mama say the Lord enters you in stages,
first like a match lit under your skin,
then like an animal biting through bone
with soft teeth. Mama say lie still
and wait for glory to consume you,
wrap its way into your map
like a lover had his finger on paradise,
knew the way with all his heart, then lost it.
I always shudder when I pray,
so your name must be a prayer.
Saying your name colors my mouth,
frees loose this river, changes my skin,
turns my spine to string. I pray all the time now.
Amen.

Try not to touch me while I tell this.
Try not to brush the thick tips of your fingers
against my throat while my throat moves
telling this story. Don't suddenly squeeze
my bare shoulder or travel your mouth
along the flat swell of my belly.
Don't bite at the hollow in my back,
whisper touch my ankles,
or match our skin like spoons.
Don't punctuate this rambling sentence
with your tongue or trace your name
on the backs of my legs,
please don't walk the question
of your breath along my thighs

or draw a map on my quivering breastbone
guiding me to you,
me to you,
me to you,
don't play me
that way

don't *play* me

that way

the way the saxman plays his woman,
blowing into her mouth till she cries,
allowing her no breath of her own.
Don't play me that way, baby, the way
the saxman plays his lady,
that strangling, soft murder—notes like bullets,
riffs like knives and the downbeat slapping
into her. and she sighs.
into her. and she cries.
into her.
and she whines like the night turning.

Let me sit here on the bar stool sipping something bitter.
Let me cross my legs,
slow like the colored girls do,
and let me feel your eyes go there.
Let me feed on glory and grow fat.

Meanwhile, lover, let's fill this wicked church with music.
Let me lean into this story, for once,
without your mouth on me. The music a lit match
under my skin and I dance,
all legs and thunderous and heels too high,

I dance cheap perfume and black nail polish.
Sharkskin congregation, heads *pressed*,
attitudes too tight, won't scream
until it gets to be too much, won't beg for mercy
until I wreck the landscape with my hips.
Bar stools filling, everybody waiting for the glory
to move through me, fill me with hosannas,
rock me with hallelujahs, to shake these bored bones.
They wait for *you*, supreme love, to pull me out
onto the dance floor, make me kick my heels above my head.
High heels 'bove my nappy head.

While they wait, I will dance with the saxman,
I will shimmer as he presses my keys.
Him and me boppin', we are *wicked* church.
So don't play, do not play, did you hear me tell you
not to play me that way?
(The way I pray to be played.)

Mama say the Lord enters you in stages
(Play me that way)
First like a lit match under your skin
(Play me that way)
Then like an animal biting through bone with soft teeth
(Play me)
Mama say lie still and wait for glory
(that way)
to consume me
(that way)
Press my keys
(that way)
Press my keys
(that way)

Don't pay me no mind, lover.
I always shudder

when I pray.

Scribe

My son, budding dreadhead, has taken a break from obsessively twisting and waxing his naps, swelling his delts, and busting rhymes with no aim, backbeat, or future beyond the common room. For want of a plumper canteen, the child has laid claim to a jailhouse vocation.

I'm the writer, Mama, he tells me.
That's what I'm known for in here.

In my kitchen, clutching the receiver, I want to laugh, because my son has always been the writer, muttering witness to the underbelly, his rebel heart over thumping, his bladed lines peppered with ready-market gangster swerve and cringing in awe of themselves. I want to laugh, but

I must commit to my focus. I must be typical, single, black, with an 18-to-30-year-old male child behind bars. How deftly I have learned the up/back of that tiring Watusi.

I guess it's a poem, he'd mutter.
Throw it away if you want.

And oh, I'd ache at what he'd done, the bottoms he'd found, the clutch he claimed on what refused to be held, the queries scraped from surface. *What are you chile?*, I'd whisper as I read. Could there be a dream just temporarily deferred wallowing in those drooping denims and triple-x sweats, could there be a poet wrapped tight against the world in those swaddling clothes?

He was the writer then, but now, reluctant resident of the Middlesex County House of Correction, he is *the* writer, sanctioned by the baddest of badasses because he has trumpeted the power of twisting verb and noun not only to say things, but to *get* shit:

They paying me to write love letters to their ladies.
I write poems if they rather have that,
this one big musclehead brother everybody be sweatin
even asked me to write a letter to his mama on her birthday.

They call him Scribe.

They bring him their imploded dreams, letters from their women-in-waiting tired of waiting. On deadline, he spins impossible sugar onto the precise lines of legal pads, pens June/moon dripping enough to melt a b-girl's hard heart. He drops to scarred knees, moans and whimpers in stilted verse, coaxing last ink from a passed-around ballpoint, making it wail:

please please babygirl,
don't be talking about not waiting out my time,
only five years left, that ain't much,
hey Scribe, Scribe, hook me up, man,
I ain't got no answer for this shit she sudden talkin.

Tattooed in riotous colors, they circle him in the common room, whispering to him beneath the surface of their reputations:

Got a job for you Scribe, got a job.

When the letters are crafted just right, copied over and over and edited for the real, the customers stumble through the aloud reading of them, scared of their own new voices. Too dazzled to demand definition, they scrunch scarred foreheads and whistle through gold caps at the three-syllable kickverbs:

I'm gon' trust you, they tell my son. *I'm gon' trust you on this.*
They don't want their softness. They don't want it.

You know, Scribe, damn, damn this shit SINGS!
You blessed man, you blessed.
I don't know what you saying man, but it sho sound good.
So I'm gon' trust you. I'm gon' trust you on this.

Then they copy the words in their own hand and send spun silk shoutouts to the freewalking world, hoping that a disillusioned girlfriend or a neglected mother or a wife-in-waiting tired of waiting will slit open the envelope and feel a warm repentant soul spill out into her hands.

And I must admit, as a fellow poet, I envy my son, this being necessary. Think of it. Which of us would refuse to try on the first face of a killer, our life teetering on every line? Wouldn't we want to craft a new front for everyone just once, to rewrite one moment of a life story, to beg for mercy on behalf of someone who has never known life on his knees?

And at the end of our flowery betrayal, that white-heat moment of no sound. In the steamy pocket of it, all we'd need is one person rising up slow, full of spit and menace, to say:

OK, OK, I'm gon' trust you on that one.
I'm gon' have to trust you on that.

What You Pray Toward

"The orgasm has replaced the cross as the focus of longing and the image of fulfillment."
—*Malcolm Muggeridge, 1966*

I.

Hubbie #1 used to get wholly pissed when I made
myself come. *I'm right here!*, he'd sputter, blood
popping to the surface of his fuzzed cheeks,
goddamn it, I'm right here! By that time, I was
in no mood to discuss the myriad merits of my
pointer, or to jam the brakes on the express train
slicing through my blood. It was easier to suffer
the practiced professorial huff, the hissed invectives
and the cold old shoulder, liver-dotted, quaking
with rage. Shall we pause to bless professors and
codgers and their bellowed, unquestioned ownership
of things? I was sneaking time with my own body.
I know I signed something over, but it wasn't that.

II.

No matter how I angle this history, it's weird,
so let's just say *Bringing Up Baby* was on the telly
and suddenly my lips pressing against
the couch cushions felt spectacular and I thought
wow this is strange, what the hell, I'm 30 years old,
am I dying down there is this the feel, does the cunt
go to heaven first, ooh, snapped river, ooh shimmy
I had never had it never knew, oh I clamored and
lurched beneath my little succession of boys I cried
writhed hissed, *ooh wee*, suffered their flat lapping
and machine-gun diddling their insistent *c'mon girl
c'mon* until I memorized the blueprint for drawing

blood from their shoulders, until there was nothing
left but the self-satisfied liquidy snore of he who has
rocked she, he who has made she weep with script.
But this, oh Cary, gee Katherine, hallelujah Baby,
the fur do fly, all gush and kaboom on the wind.

III.

Don't hate me because I am multiple, hurtling.
As long as there is still skin on the pad of my finger,
as long as I'm awake, as long as my (new) husband's
mouth holds out, I am the spinner, the unbridled,
the bellowing freak. When I have emptied him,
he leans back, coos, edges me along, keeps wondering
count. He falls to his knees in front of it, marvels
at my yelps and carousing spine, stares unflinching
as I bleed spittle onto the pillows.
He has married a witness.
My body bucks, slave to its selfish engine,
and love is the dim miracle of these little deaths,
fracturing, speeding for the surface.

IV.

We know the record. As it taunts us, we have giggled,
considered stopwatches, little laboratories. Somewhere
beneath the suffering clean, swathed in eyes and silver,
she came 134 times in one hour. I imagine wires holding
her tight, her throat a rattling window. Searching scrubbed
places for her name, I find only reams of numbers. I ask
the quietest of them:

V.

Are we God?

Dream Dead Daddy Walking

You don't have to be asleep to dream. At any time,
cue the untruths. You can believe, for instance,
that your dead father isn't dead anymore.
There is the doorbell clanging and your one-year-old
screeching *Granddaddy!*, lurching and running
to the banister to risk his life looking over,
and yes, there is a curving staircase, partially awash
in sun, and your father skipping stairs,
grinning gold tooth, growling *Hey Meathead*
to his yelping grandson. Your unslept story freezes
right here, with his bony brown face upturned,
you and your leaping baby looking down at him.
The clock locks on this.
The raucous welcome stops, he does not take
another step, nothing moves but his face,
slipping out of sun into dead again. I am alone
in my office, terrified of conjuring him,
but there is the clanging, the boy screeching,
the gold tooth, those slats of June, the son,
the father, the daughter seeing all of what has
already happened happening,
and the soft remembered thud of wingtips.

Teahouse of the Almighty

July 17, 2002, Brockton, MA

Peppermint bites at the back of the teeth,
heat prickles points on an unready tongue.
The solemn eyes of Jesus contemplate from
black light: *My child, you will conquer the spice.*
You will swallow. Every blend, from rose hip
to green, is sharp saccharine and colored
like blood. The menu, scrawled in Sharpie
on gray shirt cardboard, is blotched with
smoke, and, anyway, nothing has a price.

Splintered wood seats, carved across with
curses and desperate two-syllabled prayers,
strain to hold the quivering weight of
the devoted and the hard questions poised
by their thirst. Wherever it is not stained
or peeled back or missing, the tile floor
is scarred with sloping Scripture written
from the position of the knees—*As far as*
the east is from the west, so far hath he
removed our transgressions from us.
Men with rheumy gazes arc over teacups,
sip cleansing and penance. Their suit coats,
once special at Sears, are ironed hard,
growing too airy, inevitably brown.

The waitress, Glorie, a spit-curled kingdom,
is spritzed, flip-tongued, ripped too suddenly
from a Southern soil. She say: *'fore you ask,*
what we got here is Domino sugar, thick cream.
From a seat near the reeking john, a crinkled
alto quavers, a choir by its ownself: *I love*

the Lord, he heard my cry. Miss Glorie stops,
shows the palm of her hand to heaven.
All faith, it is believed, lies in testimony.

The voice is old church, teetering, dim-visioned,
pink foam rollers in thin, hard-oiled strands.
It is northbound Greyhound, shucked beans,
buttercake, chicken necks in waxed paper
trapped against their own oil. The voice belongs
to the m'dear of red dust, to our daily dying mothers,
to every single city's west side. It wears aged lace
and A-lines hemmed with masking tape.
The woman wails sanctified because the heat
has singed her fingers, because a huge empty
sits across from her and breathes a little death
onto the folds of her face. *I'll take another cup,*
she says. *I believe I will. But don't be scared,*
Glorie, make it hot. Put some fire under it.
Lord can't tell I'm here 'less I holla out loud.

She rocks the day dim, sips slow, props the comma
of her spine against the hard wood. But she snaps
straight whenever the door opens.
He's gon' come.
He knows the place.
A man gets thirsty.

Running for Aretha

For Louis Brown, Boston

I blew out my speakers today listening to Aretha
sing gospel. "Take My Hand, Precious Lord"
crackled and popped until finally the tweeters
smoked and the room grew silent, although,
as my mama would say, *The spirit kept kickin'.*
Humming fitfully between sips of spiced tea,
I decided that salvation didn't need a soundtrack.

Boston is holding its breath, flirting with snow.
Upstairs, plugged into M.C. somebody, my son
is oblivious to headlines. The world is a gift,
just waiting for his fingers to loose the ribbon.

He won't find out until later that a boy with his
face, his swagger, his common veil, died crumpled
on a Dorchester street. He will turn away from
tonight's filmed probings into the boy's short stay,
stutterings from stunned grandmamas,
neighbors slowly shaking their heads. He'll pretend
not to see the clip of the paramedics screaming
obscenities at the boy's heart, turning its stubborn
key with their fists. *Want anything, Ma?* he'll ask
from the kitchen, where he has skulked for shelter,
for a meal of sugar and bread to block his throat.

The crisp, metallic stench of the busted speakers
reminds me that there are other things to do.
My computer hums seductively.
My husband hints that he may want to argue about sex.
I think about starting a fire, but don't think I can stand
the way the paper curls, snaps, and dissolves into ash.

So I climb the stairs to my son's room,
rest my head against the door's cold wood,
listen to the muffled roars of rappers. But I don't knock.
He deserves one more moment of not knowing that boy's face,
how I ran to Aretha's side, how tight the ribbon is tied.

When the Burning Begins

For Otis Douglas Smith, my father

The recipe for hot water cornbread is simple—
cornmeal, hot water. Mix 'til sluggish,
then dollop into a sizzling skillet.
When you smell the burning begin, flip it.
When you smell the burning begin again,
dump it onto a plate. You've got to wait
for the burning and get it just right.

Before the bread cools down,
smear it with sweet salted butter
and smash it with your fingers,
crumple it up in a bowl
of collard greens or buttermilk,
forget that I'm telling you it's the first thing
I ever cooked, that my daddy was laughing
and breathing and no bullet in his head
when he taught me.

Mix it 'til it looks like quicksand, he'd say.
'Til it moves like a slow song sounds.

We'd sit there in the kitchen, licking our fingers
and laughing at my mother,
who was probably scrubbing something with bleach,
or watching *Bonanza*,
or thinking how stupid it was to be burning
that nasty old bread in that cast-iron skillet.
When I told her that I'd made my first-ever pan
of hot water cornbread, and that my daddy
had branded it glorious, she sniffed and kept
mopping the floor over and over in the same place.

So here's how you do it:

You take out a bowl, like the one
we had with blue flowers and only one crack,
you put the cornmeal in it.
Then you turn on the hot water and you let it run
while you tell the story about the boy
who kissed your cheek after school
or about how you really want to be a reporter
instead of a teacher or nurse like Mama said,
and the water keeps running while Daddy says
You will be a wonderful writer
and you will be famous someday and when
you get famous, if I wrote you a letter and
sent you some money, would you write about me?

and he is laughing and breathing and no bullet
in his head. So you let the water run into this mix
'til it moves like mud moves at the bottom of a river,
which is another thing Daddy said, and even though
I'd never even seen a river,
I knew exactly what he meant.
Then you turn the fire way up under the skillet,
and you pour in this mix
that moves like mud moves at the bottom of a river,
like quicksand, like slow song sounds.
That stuff pops something awful when it first hits
that blazing skillet, and sometimes Daddy and I
would dance to those angry pop sounds,
he'd let me rest my feet on top of his
while we waltzed around the kitchen
and my mother huffed and puffed
on the other side of the door. *When you are famous,*
Daddy asks me, *will you write about dancing*

in the kitchen with your father?
I say everything I write will be about you,
then you will be famous too. And we dip and swirl
and spin, but then he stops.
And sniffs the air.

The thing you have to remember
about hot water cornbread
is to wait for the burning
so you know when to flip it, and then again
so you know when it's crusty and done.
Then eat it the way we did,
with our fingers,
our feet still tingling from dancing.
But remember that sometimes the burning
takes such a long time,
and in that time,
sometimes,

poems are born.

Blood Dazzler, 2008

It was just going to be one poem—about the 34 and the growing gloom, the rising water, the pointless buttons pushed and pushed. But then someone in an audience, who'd seen a worker in the French Quarter hammering a nail into a piece of wood, says *Well, they had Mardi Gras, didn't they?* and instead of smashing the woman in the face, the poet writes a storm with dreads sodden and whipping. She writes a wild woman who is demon and goddess and mother and bitch and a turn in the weather. She writes grandmamas splayed and spinning in the muck. She writes a stanza with no words. Writers slip a medal over her head, say *This is good work, poet.* But when limelight washes over the snazzy awards, she sees a table of snarling skinheads, another table of immeasurably sad women without sons. Being poems still hasn't saved them.

Prologue—
And Then She Owns You

This is not morning. There is a nastiness
slowing your shoes, something you shouldn't step in.
It's shattered beads, stomped flowers, vomit—
such stupid beauty,

beauty you can stick a manicured finger
into and through, beauty that doesn't rely
on any sentence the sun chants, it's whiskey
swelter blown scarlet.

Call this something else. Last night it had a name,
a name wedged between an organ's teeth, a name
pumping a virgin unawares, a curse word.
Wail it, regardless.

Weak light, bleakly triumphant, will unveil scabs,
snippets of filth music, cars on collapsed veins.
The whole of gray doubt slithers on solemn skin.
Call her New Orleans.

Each day she wavers, not knowing how long she
can stomach the introduction of needles,
the brash, boozed warbling of bums with neon crowns,
necklaces raining.

She tries on her voice, which sounds like cigarettes,
pubic sweat, brown spittle lining a sax bell,
the broken heel on a drag queen's scarlet slings.
Your kind of singing.

Weirdly in love, you rhumba her edges, drink
fuming concoctions, lick your lukewarm breakfast
directly from her crust. Go on, admit it.
You are addicted

to her brick hips, the thick swerve she elicits,
the way she kisses you, her lies wide open.
She prefers alleys, crevices, basement floors.
Hell, let her woo you.

This kind of romance dims the worth of soldiers,
bends and breaks the back, sips manna from muscle,
tells you *Leave your life*. Pack your little suitcase,
flee what is rigid

and duly prescribed. Let her touch that raw space
between cock and calm, the place that scripts such jazz.
Let her pen letters addressed to your asking.
You s-s-stutter.

New Orleans's, p-please. Don't. Blue is the color
stunning your tongue. At least the city pretends
to remember to be listening.
She grins with glint tooth,

wiping your mind blind of the wife, the children.
the numb ritual of job and garden plot.
Gently, she leads you out into the darkness
and makes you drink rain.

5 p.m., Tuesday, August 23, 2005

"Data from an Air Force reserve unit reconnaissance aircraft . . . along with observations from the Bahamas and nearby ships . . . indicate the broad low pressure area over the southeastern Bahamas has become organized enough to be classified as tropical depression twelve."
  —NATIONAL HURRICANE CENTER

A muted thread of gray light, hovering ocean,
becomes throat, pulls in wriggle, anemone, kelp,
widens with the want of it. I become
a mouth, thrashing hair, an overdone eye. How dare
the water belittle my thirst, treat me as just
another
small
disturbance,

try to feed me
from the bottom of its hand?

I will require praise,
unbridled winds to define my body,
a crime behind my teeth
because

every woman begins as weather,
sips slow thunder, knows her hips. Every woman
harbors a chaos, can
wait for it, straddling a fever.

For now,
I console myself with small furies,
those dips in my dawning system. I pull in
a bored breath. The brine shivers.

"Satellite imagery ... Doppler radar data from the Bahamas and Miami ... indicate [tropical depression twelve] has become much better organized ... has strengthened into tropical storm Katrina."
 —NATIONAL HURRICANE CENTER

The difference in a given name. What the calling,
the hard K, does to the steel of me,
how suddenly and surely it grants me
pulse, petulance. Now I can do

my own choking. I can thread my fingers
with grimace and spit

zephyr, a gentle marking
of the very first time I felt

that crisp, bladed noun
in my own mouth.

5 p.m., Thursday, August 25, 2005

The National Hurricane Center upgrades tropical storm Katrina to Hurricane
Katrina.

My eye takes in so much—
what it craves, what I never hoped to see.
It doesn't care about pain, is eons away
from the ego's thump, doesn't hesitate
to scan the stark, adjust for distance,
unravel the world for no reason at all, except that it

hungers.

It needs to croon in every screeching hue,
strives to know waltz, hesitation,
small changes in sun. It spots
weeping, then wants to see its sound. It spies
pattern and restlessly hunts the solid drum.

The eye

pushes my rumbling bulk forward,
urges me to see
what it sees.

7 p.m., Thursday, August 25, 2005

Hurricane Katrina makes landfall in Florida.

I see

        what this language does

and taste

        soil on my tongue

and feel

        brick splintering spine

and hear

        them

and want it

        all

Man on the TV Say

Go. He say it simple, gray eyes straight on and watered,
he say it in that machine throat they got.
On the wall behind him, there's a moving picture
of the sky dripping something worse than rain.
Go, he say. Pick up y'all black asses and run.
Leave your house with its splinters and pocked roof,
leave the pork chops drifting in grease and onion,
leave the whining dog, your one good watch,
that purple church hat, the mirrors.
Go. Uh-huh. Like our bodies got wheels and gas,
like at the end of that running there's an open door
with dry and song inside. He act like we supposed
to wrap ourselves in picture frames, shadow boxes,
and bathroom rugs, then walk the freeway, racing
the water. *Get on out.* Can't he see that our bodies
are just our bodies, tied to what we know?
Go. So we'll go. 'Cause the man say it strong now,
mad like God pointing the way outta Paradise.
Even he got to know our favorite ritual is root,
and that none of us done ever known a horizon,
especially one that cools our dumb running,
whispering urge and constant: *This way. Over here.*

Won't Be but a Minute

Tie Luther B to that cypress. He gon' be all right.
That dog done been rained on before,
he done been here a day or two by hisself before,
and we sho' can't take him. Just leave him
some of that Alpo and plenty of water.
Bowls and bowls of water.
We gon' be back home soon this thing pass over.
Luther B gon' watch the place while we gone.
You heard the man—he said *Go*—and you know
white folks don't warn us 'bout nothing unless
they scared too. We gon' just wait this storm out.
Then we come on back home. Get our dog.

8 a.m., Sunday, August 28, 2005

Katrina becomes a Category 5 storm, the highest possible rating.

For days, I've been offered blunt slivers
of larger promises—even flesh,
my sweet recurring dream,
has been tantalizingly dangled before me.
I have crammed my mouth with buildings,
brushed aside skimpy altars,
snapped shut windows to bright shatter
with my fingers. And I've warned them, soft:
You must not know my name.

Could there be other weather,
other divas stalking the cringing country
with insistent eye?
Could there be other rain,
laced with the slick flick of electric
and my own pissed boom? Or could this be

it, finally,
my praise day,
all my fists at once?

Now officially a bitch, I'm confounded by words—
all I've ever been is starving, fluid, and noise.
So I huff a huge sulk, thrust out my chest,
open wide my solo swallowing eye.

You must not know

Scarlet glare fixed on the trembling crescent,

I fly.

The Dawn of Luther B's Best Day

Luther B, months mangy and chained down
against m'dear's shade tree, feels a little thrill
shoot through his planted paws, sniffs questions
in the swirled air. Suddenly the day is touching him.
The mutt whimpers, raps yaps, twists his stout squatness,
strains against thick links, moans a wavering O.

But nobody's coming this time, nobody to scratch
the dead skin behind his ear, no m'dear hobbling out
in scuffs and shift, cussing, carrying a fresh can a' heaven.

All that's reachin' for him now is the sky, the God daddy,
pressing down fast, cracks of purple in its fingers.
Luther B writhes on his back in the dirt, tumbling the fleas,
then forces himself still. Snout upturned, he watches
his deliverance come closer. With the first plops of rain,
he snarls low and realizes just what kinda dog he is—
itchy, utterly bitchless, locked to the skin of a tree,
but fat with future. And now a cool day comin'. Hot damn.

10:30 a.m., Sunday, August 28, 2005

Their hard-pressed hair is topped with every manner
of church hat—ski-sloped satin, velvet, or brocade crowns
adorned with glittered netting, babbling florals,
even stunned fake bluebirds. The senior choir
warms up, humming tumult away from their joints.
Caged in impossibly proper brown serge, the elders
amble to their front pews and gaze upon the preacher
with unquestioned reverence. They try not to notice how small
he really is, 'cause he's the only one there who knows Jesus
by His first name. Rev's an itty bitty somethin', though.
If they all took a deep breath and let it out in his direction,
they could lift him off his feet. They could pray for themselves.

Luther B Rides Out the Storm

Lord ham mercy, m'dear moaned,
slow and real Baptist like, every time some kink
swerved her day—an August noon sweatin'
the sugar out of her just-pressed hair,
a run in her last pair of church stockings.
Luther B sympathized with a cock of his thick head.
Now, in the looped reloop of dog thought,
he wonders about that Lord, and mercy,
and m'dear's little surrenders, surrenders.

His wet yelps and winding croon reach nothing.
Wobbling, he latches muzzle to the wall of wind.
There's got to be some good livin' at the end of this,
maybe a pork chop with some religion still hangin' from it,
or a skillet scrape of m'dear's fat oxtails and onion rice.
Bet there's daybreaks stackin' up behind those clouds,
regular, with quiet moons behind, all rowed up, ready.

The day's pewter howling wounds a rib,
darkens Luther B's itching with blood.

Paddling in frantic blue circle,
he fights his slippery chain,
treads toward a little bit more of remember—
Damn dog ain't nuthin' but trouble.
But I loves me some Luther B.
I loves him to death.

What to Tweak

Italicized excerpts are from an August 31, 2005, e-mail from Marty Bahamonde to his boss, Michael Brown, head of the Federal Emergency Management Agency. Bahamonde was one of the only FEMA employees in New Orleans at the time.

Aug. 31, 12:20 p.m. Re: New Orleans

Sir, I know that you know the situation is past critical. Here are some things you might not know.

> Rainbows warp when you curse them.
> I have held a shiver of black child against my body.
> The word *river* doesn't know edges.
> God wouldn't do this.
> There's a Chevy growing in that tree.
> Here, I am so starkly white.
> Sometimes bullets make perfect sense.
> Eventually the concrete will buckle.
> They won't stop screeching at me.
> I have passed out all my gum.
> So many people are thirsty.
> A kid breathes wet against my thigh.
> He calls me father.

Hotels are kicking people out. . . .

> No one is prepared for their sulking shadows.
> They sully sleek halls, leave smudges on grand glass.
> They double negative, sport clothes limp with ache.
> These people don't know this place,
> this costly harbor where they have always pointed,
> eyes bucked and overwhelmed,
> giddy with the conjure of mirrored silver

and whole cups dedicated to tea.
In the sudden midst of glorious this,
they fill their cavernous pockets with faith.
Why didn't we bolt the doors
before they began to dream?

thousands gathering in the streets with no food or water ...

The weakened mob veers into the open for breath.
Ashy babies bellow, B-boys hurl gold-toothed *fuck-its*,
everyone asks for food. And the heat singes art
on bare backs, sucks tears from parched skin.
It's true there is no food, but water is everywhere.
The demon has chapped their rusty ankles,
reddened the throats of babies, smashed homes to mist.
It is water that beats down without taking a breath
and points its dank mossy finger at their faith.
I have killed you, it patters.
I have bled you dry.

Hundreds still being rescued from homes.

Or not.
Death has an insistent iron smell, oversweet rot
loud enough to wither certain woods.
Behind sagging doors specters swirl,
grow huge-limbed, stink brilliance.
And up on the roofs of tombs,
sinking mothers claw the sky,
pray the rising river away from their scream.
The moon refuses to illuminate their overtures,
winking dim then winking shut.
From the papery peaks of three-flats,
shots and weeping in the starless dark.

If you listen, you can hear the dying.
It creaks odd and high,
a song slowly larger than the singer.

Evacuation in process. Plans developing for dome evacuation but hotel situation adding to problem. We are out of food and running out of water at the dome. Plans in works to address the critical need.

Stifle the stinking, shut down the cameras,
wave Dubya down from the sky.
Subtract the babies, unarm the flailers,
Hose that wailing bitch down!
Draw up a blueprint, consider detention,
throw them some cash from a bag.
Tell them it's God, ply them with preachers,
padlock the rest of the map.
Hand them a voucher, fly in some Colonel,
twist the volume knob hard.
Turn down the TV, distract them with vision,
pull out your hammer and nail.
Sponge off their shoulders, suckle their children,
prop them upright for the lens.
Tolerate ranting, dazzle with card tricks,
pin flags on absent lapels.
Try not to breathe them, fan them with cardboard,
say that their houses will rise.
Play them some music, swear you hear engines,
drape their stooped bodies with beads.
Salute their resilience, tempt them with future,
surrender your shoes to the mud.
Promise them trailers, pass out complaint forms,
draft a law wearing their names.
Say help is coming, say help is coming,
then say that help's running late.

Shrink from their clutches, lie to their faces,
explain how the levies grew thin.
Mop up the vomit, cringe at their crudeness,
audition their daughters for rape.
Stomp on their sleeping, outrun the gangsters,
pass out American flags.

DMAT staff working in deplorable conditions. The sooner we can get the medical patients out, the sooner we can get them out.

Breathing bladed, blood tinged black,
their stark diseases mystify, ooze unbridled.
Heat stuns their grip on history,
so they keep attempting to walk back
into remembered days of weather
that never grew more difficult than rain.
They crave the reign of simple delta,
when skinned pig, peppered collards,
and a bottle of red heat signaled a day gone right.
So they keep trying to walk, to force their feet
into the now-obscenity of a straight line,
to begin with that first blessing—*forward, forward,*
not getting the joke of their paper shoes,
not knowing the sidewalks are gone.

Brown:

Thanks for update. Anything specific I need to do

or tweak?

The President Flies Over

Aloft between heaven and them,

I babble the landscape—what staunch, vicious trees,
what cluttered roads, slow cars. This is my

country as it was gifted me—victimless, vast.
The soundtrack buzzing the air around my ears
continually loops ditties of eagles and oil.
I can't choose. Every moment I'm awake,
aroused instrumentals channel theme songs,
speaking
what I cannot.

I don't ever have to come down.
I can stay hooked to heaven,
dictating this blandness.
My flyboys memorize flip and soar.
They'll never swoop real enough
to resurrect that other country,

won't ever get close enough to give name
to tonight's dreams darkening the water.

I understand that somewhere it has rained.

Tankas

Never has there been
a wind like this. Its throaty
howl has memorized
my name. And it calls, and it
calls, and lamb to ax, I come.

I have three children,
but only two arms. He falls
and barely splashes,
that's how incredibly light
he is—was. How death whispers.

I lie on my back
on this roof, dazed by the stars
blazing on pure black.
I croon feverish, off-key
to drown out the water's teeth.

I found my sister
whirling in the peppered blue,
my father under rock,
and then myself, fingering
the hard barrel of a gun.

The breath just before
the last breath harbors the soul
encased in a verb.
I know the word by heart now.
Oh, I wish I could tell you.

Here is what drowning
feels like—God's hands smothering
your heart. And the thumps
grow slower, slower, until
He takes back your name. Lifts you.

Balanced on my toes,
foul panties drooped to ankles,
I scan the street, then
squeeze both of my dead eyes shut,
teeter, shit on the sidewalk.

                    Go, they said. Go. *Go.*
                    Get out before the rain comes,
                    before you can't run,
                    before the mud smells your skin
                    and begins its swirl, its hug.

What's in the water?
What nips me, sucks at my legs,
bumps and leaves bruises?
I will walk, but I won't look
at the flow that says *Stop. Rest.*

                    I see how the men
                    look at my bended body,
                    like its first rapist
                    was rain. And now they hover,
                    because I have been broken.

Can't find my rhythm,
can't pinpoint that fleeting pulse.
The drum at my core
taps stubborn single lyric,
then rimshot. I cross over.

Ethel's Sestina

*Ethel Freeman's body sat for days in her wheelchair outside the New Orleans
Convention Center. Her son Herbert, who had assured his mother that help was
on the way, was forced to leave her there once she died.*

Gon' be obedient in this here chair,
gon' bide my time, fanning against this sun.
I ask my boy, and all he says is *Wait.*
He wipes my brow with steam, says I should sleep.
I trust his every word. Herbert my son.
I believe him when he says help gon' come.

Been so long since all these suffrin' folks come
to this place. Now on the ground 'round my chair,
they sweat in my shade, keep asking my son
could that be a bus they see. It's the sun
foolin' them, shining much too loud for sleep,
making us hear engines, wheels. Not yet. Wait.

Lawd, some folks prayin' for rain while they wait,
forgetting what rain can do. When it come,
it smashes living flat, wakes you from sleep,
eats streets, washes you clean out of the chair
you be sittin' in. Best to praise this sun,
shinin' its dry shine. *Lawd have mercy, son,*

is it coming? Such a strong man, my son.
Can't help but believe when he tells us, *Wait.*
Wait some more. Wish some trees would block this sun.
We wait. Ain't no white men or buses come,
but look—see that there? Get me out this chair,
help me stand on up. No time for sleepin',

'cause look what's rumbling this way. If you sleep
you gon' miss it. *Look there*, I tell my son.
He don't hear. I'm 'bout to get out this chair,
but the ghost in my legs tells me to wait,
wait for the salvation that's sho to come.
I see my savior's face 'longside that sun.

Nobody sees me running toward the sun.
Lawd, they think I done gone and fell asleep.
They don't hear *Come.*

Come.
Come.
Come.
Come.
Come.
Come.
Ain't but one power make me leave my son.
I can't wait, Herbert. Lawd knows I can't wait.
Don't cry, boy, I ain't in that chair no more.

Wish you coulda come on this journey, son,
seen that ol' sweet sun lift me out of sleep.
Didn't have to wait. And see my golden chair?

ST. BERNARD PARISH, LA, Sept. 7 (UPI)—Thirty-four bodies were found drowned in a nursing home where people did not evacuate. More than half of the residents of St. Rita's Nursing Home, 20 miles southeast from downtown New Orleans, died August 29 when floodwaters from Hurricane Katrina reached the home's roof.

1.

I believe Jesus is hugely who He says He is:
The crook of an arm,
a shadow threatening my hair.
a hellish glare beneath the moonwash,
the slapping storm that wakes me,
the washing clean.

2.

The Reaper has touched his lips to my days,
blessing me with gray fragrance and awkward new skin.
What makes the dust of me smell like a dashed miracle,
the underside of everything?
What requires me to hear the bones?

3.

Before the rain stung like silver, I had forgotten me.
My name was a rude visitor, arriving
unannounced, without a gift,
always leaving too soon.

4.

If you knew my alley, its stink and blue,
if you knew dirt-gritted collard greens
salt-pork slick and doused with Tabasco,
then you knew me.
I know that you've come

with my engine, and the rest of my skin.
You will rise me.

5.

Son don't rise,
daughter don't know enough to dial a phone.
Gets harder to remember
how my womb folded because of them,
how all of me lumbered with their foolish weight.
See what they have done,
how hard and sweet they done dropped me here?

6.

Clumps of earth in the rising and me
too weathered to birth a howl.
I sleep in small shatters. I climb
the bitten left wall of my heart.
In all the places I fall,
it is dry.

7.

We knew we had been bred for sacrifice,
our overflow of yesterdays too wretched a nudge,
our tired hearts borderless
and already mapped for the Motherland.
We reach for the past like it is food and we are starving.
Our surfaces are scoured.
We are prepared.
We are wrapped in white.

8.

When help comes,
it will be young men smelling like cigarettes and Chevys,
muscled boys with autumn breath and steel baskets
just the right size for our souls.

To save us, they will rub our gums with hard bread.
They will offer us
water.

9.

To cool fever, rub the sickness with wet earth.
For swelling, boil a just-plucked chicken
and douse the hurt in the steam.
Always from the position of the knees,
create the savior you need.
Then
wait.

Wait.

Jesus . . . both faith and magic have failed.

10.

There is no light, no thin food moving through my arms.
Even without machines, I feel my numbers have soared.
I am a sudden second of soft leaving.
I'm cold
and I'm strapped to this country.

11.

Daughter, son, I am bursting with this.
I am straining to celebrate the links of blood.
I am wide aloud craving something shaped like you.

12.

There are no bridges.

13.

We are stunned on our scabbed backs.
There is the sound of whispered splashing,
and then this:

Leave them.

14.

*Our father
which art in heaven . . .*

15.

The walls are slithering with Bayou spit,
tears, and the badness that muddies rivers.
We flail in that sin,
alive and bended beneath a wretched Southern rain.
We sip our breath from that filthy ocean.
Only some things float.

16.

I ain't scared of no wet, no wave. I done seen more than this.
God is in *all* houses.
Just balance the huge noun of Him on your tongue.

17.

Wait with me.
Watch me sleep in this room
that looks so much like night.
I'm gon' wake up, I swear it,
to some kind of sun.

18.

19.

My name Earline
and I'm gon' say you my life—
sugar in my veins, a single cloudy eye,
and blood when I pee.
Half dead, I used to say,
I used to tell 'em *Hell, I'm already half dead.*

20.

I have forgotten how to pray,
cannot find my knees.

I want the man with my needles.
I want that sting,
those silver holes in my body, I want
my needles,
I want my sleep for days,
I wanna cheat the Reaper.

I want somebody's hand.

21.

Hallowed be thy name

22.

Hollow be *our* names.
Call us running boards, the ice man,
big band, hogshead, possum in stewing pots.
Twist our heads on our snapping necks
back to where we danced from.
Call us names that are barely necessary.

Call us those
who do not need these days.

23.

Big Easy.
I ran your green,
rolled in your red dust,
and your sun turned the white of me red
and the black of me blue.
Funny how colored I got,
how I absorbed your heat, and how you,
without flinching,
called me your child.

24.

God, we need your glitter, you know,
those wacky miracles
you do
for no reason at all?

25.

I fight the rise with all the guitar left in my throat.
Old folks got shit to say,
ain't got but a little time to say it.
We don't never die quiet.

26.

A sudden ocean of everyone's shoulders.

27.

And this scripture: *Leave them.*

28.

And I am left, no deity hovering,
no black hair on my head,
all of me thinner than when I began.

Fingers of ice climb me,
reach my dimming light,
and choke my only angel.

29.

I had the rumble hips, I tell ya.
I was sling-back and press curl
and big titties with necessary milk.
I was somebody's woman,
I was the city where the city wasn't.
Louisiana,
goddamn.
You lied to me so lush.

30.

I lost my seeing in that war.
But I ain't gonna need these old eyes for that resurrection.

That's gon' be one *hell* of a line.

I'll be the one slightly off center.
I might be facing the wrong way.

31.

They left us. Me. Him. Our crinkled hands.
They left our hard histories, our gone children and storytells.
They left the porch creaking.
They left us to our God,

but our God was mesmerized elsewhere,
watching His rain.

32.

Thy will be done.

33.

No more of us,
stunned and silent on the skin of this sea,
this thunderous wet.
We bob and bounce and spin slow,
draped in an odd sparkle.

34.

The underearth turns its face to us.

leave

      them

Buried

"We do not dig graves or put caskets into graves any longer. The decision was made and funeral homes were notified that families and funeral homes would have to supply grave-digging personnel."
—Ed Mazoue, New Orleans City Real Estate Administrator and
Person in Charge of the City's Cemeteries

There's nothing but mud. The ground looks dry and firm,
but underneath is a stew of storm. Stout shovels, rusted,
grow gummed and heavy with what I heft and rearrange.

Progress is slow.

The sun so often steams me shut, and I have to stop
to gulp sugared bites of tea,
flick away sweat with my swollen fingers,
swat hard at sluggish flies who hover,

like they know.

And when I start again, there's a rhythm to it,
some ticking jazz that gets my square hips involved.
I craft a chant purely for downbeat:
Plunge. Push. Lift. Toss it.
Plunge. Push. Lift. Toss it.
My untried muscles blaze,
joints click,
pulse clutches my chest.

Whole clocks later, I pause to relish the feat,
to marvel at the way I've compromised the earth,
how I've been that kind of God for a minute.
But only time has moved.
It's like trying to reach the next world with a spoon.

My boy would have laughed.
Daddy, you better sit down and watch some ball game,
and we'd settle, Sunday lazy,
his squirm balanced on my belly.

He needed what I was and what I wasn't.
Giggling in little language, he lobbed me the ball soft,
walked slower when I was at his side,
shared puffed white bread and purple jelly.
He waited patiently for me after dark
while I shuffled piles of books, looking for
a bedtime drama of spacemen or soldiers,
some crayoned splash to wrap his day around.

But every night, when I opened the door to his room,
all I saw
was a quivering mountain of Snoopys, Blues, and Scoobys.
Underneath them, his happy body could barely cage breath.
Giggles unleashed his toes. My line, then: *Where are yoooou?*

Plunge. Push. Lift. Toss it.

Plunge. Push. Lift. Toss—

With the dirt balanced high, screaming my shoulder,
I think hard on those nights of tussle and squeal.
I want to feel his heat and twist in my arms again.

I have to dig.

Luther B Ascends

sketched against a wearied patch
of earth,

smashed level with the mud,
smalled

by roaring days, and a sky
he trusted,

this beast
this child

Siblings

Hurricanes, 2005

Arlene learned to dance backwards in heels that were too high.
Bret prayed for a shaggy mustache made of mud and hair.
Cindy just couldn't keep her windy legs together.
Dennis never learned to swim.
Emily whispered her gusts into a thousand skins.
Franklin, farsighted and anxious, bumbled villages.
Gert spat her matronly name against a city's flat face.
Harvey hurled a wailing child high.
Irene, the baby girl, threw pounding tantrums.
José liked the whip sound of slapping.
Lee just craved the whip.
Maria's thunder skirts flew high when she danced.
Nate was mannered and practical. He stormed precisely.
Ophelia nibbled weirdly on the tips of depressions.
Philippe slept too late, flailing on a wronged ocean.
Rita was a vicious flirt. She woke Philippe with rumors.
Stan was born business, a gobbler of steel.
Tammy crooned country, getting the words all wrong.
Vince died before anyone could remember his name.
Wilma opened her maw wide, flashing rot.

None of them talked about Katrina.
She was their odd sister,
the blood dazzler.

Uncollected 1990–2010

First Time Trying to Say Where My Son Was

I.

Who was that smoldering child with bumpy dreaded crown
and drip sex walk, slouching denims with airy ass backing
his knees, unlaced Adidas flopping, swallowing his socks?
Who was that rumbling speak, silverfish smile, cocked arm
with the witless burn of street riding the high muscle?
Who was that bobbing Adam's apple, that uncorked steam,
chiseled chest wall? Who shoved my son into this thing?

II.

The coolest mom ever, I whipped Transformers into semis
with flash fingers, memorized their campy names, spent
hours playing *soar and whoosh* with an 8½-foot GI Joe
aircraft carrier that I can't remember affording. I was tickle
monster, boogiebear, crafter of fantastical bedtime stories,
and your first stumbling dance partner while Lil' Stevie
bounced us. Where in your life did your rhythm get lost?
(You still dance like a white boy trying to dance like a black
boy when he's makin' *fun* of white boys.) And you were

the most beautiful son, riotous naps and loopy grin, sailing
through times tables and vowels, conquering that book
City Fun, bellowing it over and over at three, way
before little colored boys were supposed to know words:

Look at us go.
We have to work at this.
Here is something
to look at.
See it go up.
Up, up, up.
And look at this.

It will come down.
Down, down, down.

I was so hard willing you strength, so busy standing
at your side that I couldn't catch you when you

fell

I

didn't even hear Chicago—
Go ahead, let her be your sister
I'll be your mama

III.

My house is on fire and my baby is in the house, my house is on fire and
my baby is, my house is on fire and my children

are in the house

of correction

being corrected

During visits, I touch my mouth to the glass separating us,
spy a man blurred beneath hills of manufactured muscle.
Mama, I think they're going to kill me in here.

My house is on fire and my children are in the house.
My house is on fire and my children are in the house.
My house is on fire and my children—

What's that smell?

My house is on fire and my children are in the house
My house is on fire and your children are in the house

My womb is prepared for this. If my son is killed in his cell,
I will birth him again, already equipped with ankle cuffs,
ready to be chained to something, anything—an idea, a wall,
even a man who could be his twin. I am a huge excuse, a resolution
machine, a shackled poet with my past chained to my hands

what she know,
her boy in jail anyway

We introduced our children to the heat. We left them in the house
behind locked doors, mistook their first screams for singing,
popped our hips in the club while television slapped a blur
on their souls and taught them fuck, shame and firepower.
Escape was improbable. They were chained to each other
and every link was on fire
What sparked the flame
Who lit the match
What sparked the flame
Who lit the match

My house is on fire and my children are in the house
My house is on fire and my children are in the house
My house is on fire and my children are in the house

I don't care
who brings the water

IV.

They call it jail muscle.

You are impossibly huge on top, your biceps balloons, your head
looks so wrong teetering on your neck, I have to pull in a breath
before I can attempt my arms around you, but I cannot link my
fingers behind your back. I wonder what lives there in that small
span that I cannot reach. I wonder if that's where yesterday is

or was

Upon closer inspection, I see the sloppiness in all of you,
the construction that was ignored or abandoned, the petulant
pout of your belly, stringy calves, a tooth that aches because
it is empty inside. You are huff and puff, repetitions and iron,
all of you is the result of boredom. After two years of separate
cages, I stand across a room from you, weighing the option
to touch or not touch, and that first hug is awkward, difficult,
an utter mess because you have so boldly outgrown the arc
of my arms. You speak in uncertain solos, as if you are learning
language from its very first page:
Huh. Yeah. I. Guess. So. No. I. You. See. How. Big. My.
Arms. Are? I am a fool to your fool. Yes. I. See. You.
Are. So. Big. I. Don't. Know. How. To.

hold you.

Veins have burst beneath your skin. You have exploded, gotten
so wide. You look as if you are straining to become a wall.
I imagine under it, my son, thrashing, screaming for me, clawing
through blood and fat and gristle toward my failed embrace,
needing me as much as I need

him

you

Now I recognize only sections of you. Smile cast downward.
Reddish brown skin, history's mark in your blood, half steps
instead of whole ones. Clipped laugh, remembering.

*Ma, remember when we used to watch Transformers? Remember the first book I
ever read? You still have it? Remember how hard it used to be to comb my hair?
Remember how I used to have to wear a jacket and tie to school? Remember that
time I went skiing? When that famous man took my picture? Remember when I
got beat up that time? Remember? Remember? Remember? You remember, right?
Remember Re—*

Let

me in somewhere. Ask me to shave your head, to sweep on hot
lather and cringe as the blade scrapes you clean. Let me touch my lips
to the booming on your skin. Make me read you our story of pretend
triumphs and back alleys and Transformers and stumble dance
and coughing and dead batteries and the girl who wanted to be your sister

And look at this
It will come down
Down,
down,
down

and at the end of that story let us be standing here, my arms around
you, my fingers straining to meet behind your back. I will never
stop trying to complete this holding. I need to be completely around
you, Damon, so that all of you is within the mother circle of me
and giving you up to this world
is a choice I have yet to make.

The Blood Sonnets

I. *Me, age 12*

Sure that I was dying, that I'd died,
that the gush of iron smell and black
thick splash signaled all my sin gone wide,
I pried open the thin, wobbly back
of a record cabinet and crammed
my underwear inside. My mother had told
me nothing about my body, damned
to swell, sprout hair, creak, bleed toward old,
so I hid the stiff, soiled Carter's there
among the Coltrane, wedged wrong in all
that dangerous jazz and blues I didn't dare
dance to. Gangly gal, I was still small,
but too plumped to rest in my mama's lap.
Stashing my music, I braced for her slap.

II. *You and I, too long ago*

Brash adulterous fools, you and I
clash in a rented bed, this tryst ill-
conceived, the longed-for coupling off by
days. I bleed so much it seems a kill
has taken place, my body grieving
its harbor of woman, but do we
slow, think, push apart, stop? No. Believing
this chaos fated, we're slow to see
the sheets wide-streaked, scarlet, the fat drops
peppering carpet, my thighs burned red,
until you deadpan, *Let's call the cops.*
Looks like murder. Someone must be dead.
Spent in the midst of our vicious crime,
we phone other lives, lie about time.

III. *To her, yesterday*

The purplish clot fascinated you,
didn't it? The way blood woke you and
trembled in your jammies like a clue
you hadn't asked for. You slid your hand
inside the cleft, wiggled fingers stained
with *new me, grandma!* We rose that night
and sistered for hours. Questions rained—
Where's the egg?—and answers were your right
and my relief. I took final stock:
Age 11, size 8 feet, my height.
Oh God, my girl, my woman, the shock
of sweet you lurching forward just might
kill me. Let's ignore the creeping sands.
Let's laugh and clasp each other's bloody hands.

It Creeps Back In

before i can narrow my focus, before i can
bankroll a liturgy that qualifies as tribal,
i gulp gin and sitting water. i go rigid in front
of an unplugged fridge, spraying butter into
my mouth. brushing dead hair into the sink,
i listen while my blustering cell whispers
weather, weather, weather. it's an alternate
tuesday, so i jump a madison st. bus toward
my *uh-uhing* white savior, board-certified,
schooled in the lustful coo of the racially
aware: *so, tell me, are you still sleeping all
day?* yes, i'm trapped in that thrash where
i struggle to paint my slut shut. yes, i must
insist on settling my bill with a wig reveal.
yes, i howl at bullseye. *depression, especially
in its dreary black woman version, should
NOT be ignored*, he warns, and that tenet
duly rouses the wee pink rituals of my south.
in the ladies' room, i rock back on a hipbone,
enter myself with a snaking finger. again
i'm mightily awed by the ghost of current.
i'm now the weather. i can make the rain.
i can make the rain say *you still need me.*
i can make it lie in the voice of my mother.

The Episode Where Daddy Dies—but, Again, Doesn't

Between sprays of Arkansas invective, my father
begs for charred chicken necks, a pickled pig foot
splashed with Tabasco, collards drooped with oil.
Groaning at the hospital's affected white food,
stuff that *colored folks don't know nuthin' 'bout*, he
whines and whines a decided preference for meals
of slow but yummy murder. Instead, his machine-
booty-ed nurse—who was probably named Bertha
before anyone was named anything—slams down
his Tuesday entree, an arid puck of cordon bleu
he ruefully pokes, releasing a cold, sluggish
stream of butter. *This ain't what I want.* Bertha nods
dutifully, pretends to take another order on a tiny
notepad. My father actually believes she's finally
given in. *Bring me sardines, saltines and hot sauce,*
and some collards. Chicken necks. "So let me get
this straight, Otis," Bertha coos, "you want me to
help kill you?" Daddy's eyes widen at this hippy
gal's suggestion that he might actually end, that
the stuff what grew him up can put him under.

Hooked to a rusted bracket in the room's clean sky,
a flickering Philco spins the action-crammed tale
of a wily cartoon cat obsessed with a little rat.
Daddy goes on and on about a rat he once sparred
with in our westside Chicago walkup—*Slowed*
his little ass down with a hammer—and guffaws
as Tom is bloodlessly blown askew and two times
resurrected, jaunty hat back in place over his ears,
his bowtie fluffed, his day going on. *Didn't take*
but two blows with that hammer, just two blows.

No one's sure just why Daddy's here. A fitful thud
boogies the length of his sunken belly, a warning
or introduction to a thing unblessed, and the rotted
pocket between his gold and real teeth whistles
for religion. Bertha sighs as she struggles with
thin veins and gummy, grappling blood, measures
his timid daily dribble of piss. Both of us wait for
my mother, who never visits, to visit, but when she
does, her nose scrunches, she doesn't sit or touch
anything, she is perfectly at the edge of the room.
While Bertha delicately sponges the ashed length
of her complaining husband, my mother locks her
eyes on the stuttering TV screen, cheering silently
for the rat to die, die, she is on the edge of her seat
sighing as the spry rodent ricochets back to breath.

To the Woman, Not Trying to Fly, Who Fell with Her Legs Closed, Arms Pressed Against the Front of Her Body, While Primly Clutching Her Purse

September 11, 2001

I.

You didn't topple, cartwheel or plummet. You believed
that your descent, while swift, would end tenderly,
and that there would then be things to attend to.
While others fell past you, screeching for mercy
and splayed like stars, you aimed your pinpoint of body
toward a future that included your checkbook,
snapshots of squirming children,
a scarlet stump of lipstick.
There would be need for these things again.
Your keenly ordered mind couldn't help but see the vertical
drop as mere inconvenience. You didn't wing or flounder.
Your eyes straight ahead, your sweet drumming heart
struggling toward a fuss, you were most concerned with decorum,
the proper way for a lady to manage adversity.

There will be someone to help you to your feet,
to brush strands of the sky from your eyes.

II.

For poets, these are impossible days.
We have at our disposal every letter of every syllable
of every word ever written or spoken in any language,
but when we attempt to conjure *fly*
we so often fall.

The man with his skin fused to his shirt.
Perhaps he can tell us why.

There are hands, shoes, cell phones, sudden gifts
in the grit and rubble. Maybe they hold a clue.

There is that blue Toyota Camry sitting for nine days
in the train station lot in Tarrytown, there is *have you
seen him her them he was she is brown eyes limp tattoo*,
there are those thousands of mothers suddenly convinced
that their children had somehow learned to (*fly*),
and chose that one special moment
to do so

III.

My granddaughter is obsessed with the drawing of stars.
Each point must be perfect, meticulously measured,
twinkling beyond all reason. We have experimented
with the most efficient ways to manufacture whole
crayoned parades of starlight. We fill entire pages
with nighttime skies where no fiery wink is allowed to flaw.

"Why are you so worried about how the stars look?" I ask.
Grandmaaaa, she says, in that slow exasperated whine
that makes me feel feeble and clueless and utterly loved.

*A star has got to be perfect
before God lets it fall.*

Man, Roll the Window Down!

Inauguration Day, 2008

On a slushed side street in the Bronx, an unswerving hustler
attacks your smudged windshield with enterprise, sloshes
the pane with dusty water and rocks a feverish squeegee

before you can mouth the word *No*. Stuck at a sluggish
stoplight, you have no choice but to force a smile and nod
while he stretches the zealous machine of his body across

your hood and whips the gritty soup round and around.
It's a second before you notice that his mouth is moving,
that although he leapt to his task without warning, he is

now attempting to converse as men do, to pass the time,
to shoot the shit. You avoid the mouth, choosing instead
to scan the dank street for anything. There is lots to see—

stands tiled with threadbare skullcaps, shuttered houses
of praise, the fragrant entrance to Chicken, Ribs & Such,
the butcher shop with price tags pinned to sick meat.

A city-assed woman drills her stilettos into concrete.
But soon you run short of diversion. He's still draped
across your Corolla, swabbing, squeaking dry, mouthing.

Damned insistent now, he thumps on your windshield
and the light has changed and behind you drivers toot
their elegant *fuck you*s. You scramble for your wallet

because damn it, that's right, hell, you gotta pay the guy
for the gray crisscross swiping that dims the chaos
just enough. But what's the message of that mouth,

he needs you to know something, inside the huge O
of his wild miming there's a collision of collapsed teeth
and you slide your window down to a symphony of horn

and pissed street spittle, and your hustler's message,
what he had to get across before he let you pull away
from that street light, *Obama! Obama! Obama! Obama!*

he spurt screeches, his eyes fevered with whiskey
and damn-it-all, no verbs or adornment, just *Obama!*
as if his scrubbing little life is stuck on triumph, as if

that's all anybody needs to know this day and as he
leans in, on replay screech with his one-word stanza,
you notice that every single one of those teeth, tilted

and pushing for real estate in his mouth, every single
one of them is a gold like you've never seen before.

Post-Racial

It is wrenching, really, the way I have to take
his head in my hands and say *Baby, something
will happen soon.* The reckless of us will slap
someone's expected 'round. Our threaded
mismatched fingers screech *This tilted life.*
Lover, I am bomb-hued, napped, savvy about
the way this world sedates and separates.
When I was four, my nana wrapped around me,
whispered *lynch* directly into my ear, read me
Emmett Till's imploded eye like a bedtime
story. When I tell my lover the tale, changing
the names to protect the deluded, it fails to
daze his democratic hum. He nods heartily
and mistakes the bloodied moral for a bluish
ballad peppered with a soil he thinks he knows.

Yes, I will regret his eyes when *nigger* blurs
the air from the lowered window of a passing car,
when a colored elder strolling by sets blaze to us.
But tonight my white man makes me tea. He dips
a splintered thumb in peppermint, brushes a cool
line along the cleft of my tongue. We fold slow
into a single chair, writhe purposefully to insistent
moonwash and a new-age embarrassment of bells.
Our two huge dogs bound in, gasping, dripping
a gray rain. They shake out parties. Our home
sighs its locks shut, siphons our tangle of hue.

Second Time Trying to Say Where My Son Was

I.

And I have to decide to answer. When I click
to pick up, this is the way it goes. There's that blip
of echoed air and I say *hello, hello?* before his new
mama, disembodied white female middle American

all-purpose monotone, informs me I have a collect call
from an inmate of the Middlesex House of Corrections.
And in the silence left open for his name, my son barks
Damon! gravel and guttural and studied badass, and *oh,*

I realize, blindwalking into what now passes for ritual,
it's just my son again, his cage gracelessly unlatched
so that he can mumble, reach temporarily into other air.
My cellie says he's going to kill me in my sleep.

Then I'm just another drooped mama in a ceaseless
snaking line, summoning my cinematic coo (lately,
everyone's child is always, always about to be murdered).
Only seconds later, I'm treated to a blow-by-blow

chronicle of the shaving of his head, the sloppy gouge
when the distracted barber's razor dug deep, and *mama,
ha, ha, there was blood everywhere, but it look all right
now. Wait till you see, I'm baldheaded!* In the next breath,

I'm scared. Mama, I'm sick. I cough all night. Then,
as if he hadn't just swift-whispered that weakness, he shifts
to a sputter of jailhouse legalese, bringing me up to date
on his creaky version of hope—*since I never been in jail*

before and since I been staying out of trouble in here
and since I been doing everything they say and since it
wasn't my gun—but does it matter what grace the system
grants, if he's eating well or wrong, if the sentences run

together or top of one another, if he's crazy about his
mama? Because when dark drops and my son can no
longer fight sleep, a man, savagely focused, will arc
over him, hefting a sock swollen with dead D batteries

again. Because of the dozens of times he swears it's
about to happen, I've become an expert at visioning my
son's already nicked skull collapsing and slick with itself.
Two hundred miles away, I wince, gamely wear his wound.

II.

There's a picture of Damon, snapped over twenty years ago
when he was 2. It's black and white, just one unkempt
moment in the life of a kid, a snap only a mother craving
an unburdened memory could love. His gray sweatsuit

is caked with grime, his crown impossibly kinked. Staring
at the photo, I long to plunge my hands into those raucous
naps, kiss his nose and scoop his resisting wriggle
into my arms to snort that rusty meld of sugar and funk.

A voice interrupts. *Ma, Ma?*
It is twenty years later again.
I should have never picked up the phone.

III.

I can get in my car and drive toward him, filling three
highway hours with Motown's begging men, brown liquor
Aretha songs, and those damned insistent pictures of my
boy the way he used to be—deadpan jokester, giggling

gumcracker, stupefied by rockets and girls. Then, without
mercy, he sprouts upward, dons cavernous denims, stows
away screw-top wine and morphs into OG, cocked cannon,
baby maker, rhymebuster, lemming, lemming, lemming.

The last picture, the one of him I hate the most, stays with
me the longest—there's the grasping whiner who *really*
needs canteen money but never thanks me for raising his
four-year-old daughter. He's the single-syllable grunt, head
scarred, grossly swollen from prison workouts, who I
avoid mentioning to friends whose sons are waving grad
school acceptance letters or touring France with their jazz
bands. The most I will let on: *He's in Boston, on his own.*

I don't say: *He's locked up, but the phone rings sometimes.*

IV.

The waiting rooms are always too hot. I don't lift my eyes
often, but when I do, I see faces that mirror my own. Our
whole bodies sigh and sigh. We are in sweatshirts and jeans,
graying hair pulled back, eyes straight ahead, waiting for

our sons on the fresh-air side of bulletproof glass. A buzzer
sounds and a door slides open for their strained parade.
They shuffle as if shackled by boredom, plump and sinew
swathed in jumpsuits the color of storm. They are missing

molars, sudden bellies, downcast gaze, gang love scorched
into biceps. Numbed and innocent, numbed and guilty,
they stream in, scanning the drab room for mama or bae
or m'dear or maybe somebody, anybody, from the block,

somebody who remembers them free. Like toddlers, they
hug awkwardly, check out who else has come to see

who else, slyly size up their tribe, and greedily eye
the vending machines, broken and bulging with poisons.

I scour faces, wonder if my son's homicidal cellmate has
allowed him dawn. And then there he is. Damon, damn
him, serves up that grin, guaranteed to slap my heart open.
He sputters a few words, *See how big my arms are getting?*,

then shuts to a silence, waiting for mama to come through,
mutter a flimsy bandage, make it all better. Looking down
the long, sorrowful row, I see that expectant hush repeated,
repeated. All those mothers wanting desperately to be there

but wishing they hadn't come. If only we'd stayed home,
letting the phone ring and ring and not picking up. We could
just keep staring from our own cells into the next dawn,
loving the disappeared, and waiting for our sons to rise.

Shoulda Been Jimi Savannah, 2012

Her students always start their writing with *I feel* or *I need* or *I think* or *I want* or *I see* and she tells them to wait, wait, go out and get your hearts smashed and shattered, watch someone you love die, get hit by a Chrysler when you step into an intersection, lose clutch on a dream—*then* come back and write the "I." Her daddy wanted her to have that remarkable name Jimi and Mama nixed that damn foolishness, but the poet wears it anyway when it's time to piece together who she is. Her "I" is west-side tenement, the toxic anarchy of roach bombs. Hogshead cheese splashed with Tabasco. Clothesline jump rope whip scars. Riverview dunk tank Negroes. Tobacco stuck in her daddy's toothbrush. Steady scrawny and craving. Motown baby. Richard Speck and his pocked face. Vietnam on the TV. Mama pinching her wrong nose *hard*. The "I" wrenches open a wound. The "I" is a flurry of punches to her face. The poet is terrified, but she is writing and she is not blinking. The poet is terrified, but she writes.

How Mamas Begin Sometimes

For my mother, Annie Pearl Smith

Raging tomgirl, blood dirt streaking her thick ankles
and bare feet, she is always running, screech raucous,
careening, dare and games in her clothesline throat.
Playing like she has to play to live, she shoves at what
slows her, steamrolls whatever damn thing won't move.
Aliceville, Alabama's no fool. It won't get in her way.

Where's that girl going? Past slant sag porches, pea shuck,
twangy box guitars begging under purple dayfall. Combs
spitting sparks, hair parted and scalps scratched, mules
trembling the back road, the marbled stares of elders
fixed on checkerboards. Cursed futures crammed into
cotton pouches with pinches of bitterroot, the horrid parts
of meat stewed sweet and possible. And still, whispers
about the disappeared, whole souls lost in the passage.

Frolicking blindly, flailing tough with cousins, sisters,
but running blaze, running on purpose, bounding toward
away. She can't tag this fever, but she believes it knows
her, owns her in a way religion should. Toes tap, feet
flatten out inside the sin of shoes. She is most times
asking something, steady asking, needing to know,
needing to know *now*, taking wing on that blue restless
that drums her. Twisting on rusty hinge, that old porch door
whines for one long second 'bout where she was.

But that girl gone.

Still Life with Toothpick
For my father, Otis Douglas Smith,
and the grandparents I never knew

Maybe his father grunted, brusque and focused as he
brawled with the steering, maybe there was enough time
for a flashed invective, some hot-patched dalliance with God.
Then the Plymouth, sounding like a cheated-on woman,
screamed into hurtled revolt and cracked against a tree.

Bone rammed through shoulder, functions imploded,
compounded pulse spat slow thread into the road.
His small stuttering mother's body braided up sloppy
with foliage and windshield, his daddy became
the noon's smeared smile. For hours, they simply rained.

It is Arkansas, so the sky was a cerulean stretch, the sun
a patient wound. The boxy sedan smoldered and spat
along the blistered curve while hounds and the skittering
sniffed the lumping red river and blood birds sliced lazy over
the wreck, patiently waiting for the feast to cool. The sheriff

sidled up, finally, rolled a toothpick across his bottom teeth,
weighed his options. It was 'round lunchtime, the meatloaf
on special, that slinky waitress on call. He climbed
back into his cruiser and drove off, his mind clear. *Awfully nice*
of those poor nigras to help out. Damned if they didn't
just drip right into the dirt. Pretty much buried themselves.

Keep Saying Heaven and It Will

Otis is orphan in a very slow way. Relatives orbit the folded him, paint his parents to breath with stories that take the long way around trees, stories about the time before the two of them set out in the rumbling Plymouth, going somewhere, not getting there.

Otis is orphan in a very one way. Only one him. Only the solo with only happy stories to hear, no one says *car*. No one says *crash* or *never* or *dead now*. Everyone says *heaven*. They pat his head with flat hands, say *heaven* with all their teeth, say *heaven* with their shredding silk throats. They say *heaven heaven heaven* while their eyes rip days down.

Otis is orphan in a very wide way. They feed him dripping knots of fatback, bowlfuls of peppered collards, cheap chicken pieces sizzled thick and doughy, stewed shards of swine. They dip bread in bowls of melted butter, fry everything, okra and tomatoes, fish skin, gizzards, feet. And the women shovel sugar and coconut meat into baking pans, slosh sweet cream into bowls and stir and bake and it is all everything for him for his little empty gut. They feed him enough for two other people, though no one says *two other people*.

Finally someone says *bodies*. Something about the souls having left them and thank God for that. Someone says *maybe just one casket*. He is eating peaches drifting in a syrup. They think he is a little boy too overloved to hear. But he knows days. And this new sound, *orphan*, which means that mama and daddy are too close to be pulled apart. They are in one pretty place. But only one him, too adored and fattened. There will be a home for them to come back to. He is widening, practicing with his arms. He will be their first warm wall.

Fixing on the Next Star

Between 1916 and 1970, more than half a million African-Americans left the South and migrated to Chicago.

Mamas go quietly crazy, dizzied by the possibilities
of a kitchen, patiently plucking hairs from the skin
of supper. Swinging children from thick forearms,
they hum stanzas riddled with Alabama hue and promises
Jesus may have made. Homes swerve on foundations
while, inside, the women wash stems and shreds of syrup
from their palms and practice contented smiles,
remembering that it's a sin to damn this ritual or foul
the heat-sparkled air with any language less than prayer.

And they wait for their loves, men of marbled shoulders
and exploded nails, their faces grizzled landscapes
of scar and descent. These men stain every room
they enter, drag with them a stench of souring iron.
The dulled wives narrow their eyes, busy themselves
with clanging and stir, then feed the sweating
soldiers whole feasts built upon okra and the peppered
necks of chickens. After the steam dies, chewing
is all there is—the slurp of spiced oil, the crunch
of bone, suck of marrow. And then the conversation,
which never changes, even over the children's squeals:
They say it's better up there, it begins, and it is always
the woman who says this, and the man lowers his head
to the table and feels the day collapse beneath his shirt.

Annie Pearl, Upward

Chicago. She's heard the craving out loud, the tales of where money runs like water and after you arrive it takes—*what, a minute?*—to forget that Alabama ever held sweet for you.

She wants to find a factory that works ritual into her knuckles. She's never heard a siren razor the dark. She wants Lucky Strikes, a dose of high life every Friday, hard lessons from a jukebox. Wants to wave bye to her mama. All she needs is a bus ticket, a brown riveted case to hold her gray dress, and a waxed bag crammed with smashed slices of white bread and fat fried slabs of perch. With the whole of her chest, she knows what she's been running toward.

Apple cheek and glory gap-tooth fills the window of the Greyhound. For the upcoming, she has hot-combed her hair into shiver strings and donned a fresh-stitched skirt that wrestles with her curves. This deception is what the city asks. Her head is full and hurting with future until the bus arrives. She stumbles forth with all she owns, wanting to be romanced by some sudden thunder. She tries not to see the brown folks—the whipcloth shoe shiners, the bag carriers—staring at her, searching for some sign, aching for a smell of where she came from.

How does a city sway when you've never seen it before? It's months before she realizes that no one knows her name. No one says *Annie Pearl* and means it.

She crafts a life that is dimmer than she'd hoped, in a tenement with walls pressing in hard and fat roaches, sluggish with Raid, dropping into her food, writhing on the mattress of her Murphy bed. In daytime, she works in a straight line with other women, her hands moving without her. Repeat. Repeat. When her evenings are breezy and free and there is jiggling in her purse, she looks for music that hurts, cool slips of men in sharkskin suits, a little something to scorch her throat. Drawn to the jukebox, she punches one letter, one number, and "This Bitter Earth" punches her back, with its sad indigo spin. Dinah settles like storm over her shoulders. And she weeps when she hears what has happened to homemade guitars. How they've forgotten to need the Southern moon.

Shoulda Been Jimi Savannah

My mother scraped the name Patricia Ann from the ruins
of her discarded Delta, thinking it would offer me shield
and shelter, that leering men would skulk away at the slap
of it. Her hands on the hips of Alabama, she went for flat
and functional, then siphoned each syllable of drama,
repeatedly crushing it with her broad, practical tongue
until it sounded like an instruction to God, not a name.
She wanted a child of pressed head and knocking knees,
a trip-up in the doubledutch swing, a starched pinafore
and peppermint-in-the-sour-pickle kinda child, stiff-laced
and unshakably fixed on salvation. *Her* Patricia Ann
would never idly throat the Lord's name or wear one
of those thin, sparkled skirts that flirted with her knees.
She'd be a nurse or a third-grade teacher or a postal drone,
jobs requiring alarm-clock discipline and sensible shoes.
My four downbeats were music enough for a vapid life
of butcher-shop sawdust and fatback as cuisine, for Raid
spritzed into the writhing pockets of a Murphy bed.
No crinkled consonants or muted hiss would summon me.

My daddy detested borders. One look at my mother's
watery belly, and he insisted, as much as he could insist
with her, on the name Jimi Savannah, seeking to bless me
with the blues-bathed moniker of a ball breaker, the name
of a grown gal in a snug red sheath and unlaced All-Stars.
He wanted to shoot muscle through whatever I was called,
arm each syllable with tiny weaponry so no one would
mistake me for anything other than a tricky whisperer
with a switchblade in my shoe. I was bound to be all legs,
a bladed debutante hooked on Lucky Strikes and sugar.
When I sent up prayers, God's boy would giggle and consider.

Daddy didn't want me to be anybody's surefire factory,
nobody's callback or seized rhythm, so he conjured
a name so odd and hot even a boy could claim it. And yes,
he was prepared for the look my mother gave him when
he first mouthed his choice, the look that said, *That's it,
you done lost your goddamned mind.* She did that thing
she does where she grows two full inches with righteous,
and he decided to just whisper *Love you, Jimi Savannah*
whenever we were alone, re- and rechristening me the seed
of Otis, conjuring his own religion and naming it me.

A Colored Girl Will Slice You If You Talk Wrong About Motown

The men and women who coupled, causing us, first
arrived confounded. Surrounded by teetering towers
of *no, not now*, and *you shoulda known better*, they
cowered and built little boxes of Northern home,
crammed themselves inside, feasted on the familiar
of fat skin and the unskimmed, made gods of doors.
When we came—the same insistent bloody and question
we would have been down South—they clutched us,
plumped us on government cereal drenched in Carnation,
slathered our hair, faces, our fat wiggling arms and legs
with Vaseline. We shined like the new things we were.
The city squared its teeth, smiled oil, smelled the sour
each hour left at the corner of our mouths. Our parents
threw darts at the day. They romanced shut factories,
waged hot battle with skittering roaches and vermin,
lumbered after hunches. Their newborn children grew
like streetlights. We grew like insurance payments.
We grew like resentment. And since no tall sweetgum
thrived to offer its shouldered shade, no front porch
lesson spun wide to craft our wrong or righteous,

our parents loosed us, into the crumble, into the glass,
into the hips of a new city. They trusted exploded
summer hydrants, scarlet licorice whips, and crumbling
rocks of government cheese to conjure a sort of joy,
trusted joy to school us in the woeful limits of jukeboxes
and moonwash. Freshly dunked in church water, slapped
away from double negatives and country ways, we were
orphans of the North Star, dutifully sacrificed, our young
bodies arranged on sharp slabs of boulevard. We learned
what we needed, not from our parents and their rumored
South, but from the gospel seeping through the sad gap

in Mary Wells's grin. Smokey slow-sketched pictures
of our husbands, their future skins flooded with white light,
their voices all remorse and atmospheric coo. Little Stevie
squeezed his eyes shut on the soul notes, replacing his
dark with ours. Diana was the bone our mamas coveted,
the flow of slip silver they knew was buried deep beneath
their rollicking heft. Every lyric, growled or sweet from
perfect brown throats, was instruction: *Sit pert, pout, and
seamed silk. Then watch him beg.* Every spun line was
consolation: *You're such a good girl. If he has not arrived,
he will.* Every wall of horn, every slick choreographed
swivel, threaded us with the rhythm of the mildly wild.
We slept with transistor radios, worked the two silver knobs,
one tiny earbud blocking out the roar of our parents' tardy
attempts to retrieve us. Instead, we snuggled with the Temps,
lined up five pretty men across. And damned if they didn't
begin every one of their songs with the same word: *Girl.*

Tavern. Tavern. Church. Shuttered tavern,

then Goldblatt's, with its finger-smeared display windows full
of stifled plaid pinafore and hard-tailored serge, each unattainable
thread cooing the delayed lusciousness of layaway, another church

then, of course, Jesus pitchin' a blustery bitch on every other block,
then the butcher shop with, hard to believe, the blanched, archaic head
of a hog propped upright to lure waffling patrons into the steamy

innards of yet another storefront, where they drag their feet through
sawdust and revel in the come-hither bouquet of blood, then a vacant
lot, then another vacant lot, right up against a shoe store specializing

in unyielding leather, All-Stars and glittered stacked heels designed
for the Christian woman daring the jukebox, then the what-not joint,
with vanilla-iced long johns, wax lips crammed with sugar water,

notebook paper, swollen sour pickles buoyant in a splintered barrel,
school supplies, Pixy Stix, licorice whips, and vaguely warped 45s
by Fontella Bass or Johnnie Taylor, now oooh, what's that blue pepper

piercing the air with the nouns of backwood and cheap Delta cuts—
neck and gizzard, skin and claw—it's the chicken shack, wobbling
on a foundation of board, grease riding relentless on three of its walls,

the slick cuisine served up in virgin white cardboard boxes with Tabasco
nibbling the seams, scorched wings under soaked slices of Wonder,
blind perch fried limp, spiced like a mistake Mississippi don' made,

and speaking of, July moans around a perfect perfumed tangle of eight
Baptist gals on the corner of Kedzie and Warren, fanning themselves
with their own impending funerals, fluid-filled ankles like tree trunks

sprouting from narrow slingbacks, choking in Sears's best cinnamon-
tinged hose, their legs so unlike their arms and faces, on the other side
of the street is everything they are trying to be beyond, everything

they are trying to ignore, the grayed promise of government, twenty-five floors
of lying windows, of peeling grates called balconies, of yellow panties
and shredded diapers fluttering from open windows, of them nasty girls

with wide avenue hips stomping doubledutch in the concrete courtyard,
spewing their woman verses, too fueled and irreversible to be not
listened to and wiggled against, and the Madison Street bus revs its tired

engine, backs up a little for traction and drives smoothly into the sweaty
space between their legs, the only route out of the day we're riding through.

An All-Purpose Product

What surfaces can I use this product on?
ANSWER: Lysol may be used on hard, nonporous surfaces throughout your home. Lysol cleans, disinfects, and deodorizes regular and nonwax floors, nonwood cabinets, sinks, and garbage pails. For painted surfaces, it is recommended that the product first be tested in a small inconspicuous area.

Can Lysol be used in the kitchen?
ANSWER: Lysol may be used on countertops, refrigerators, nonwood cabinets, sinks, stovetops, and microwave ovens. For the bathroom, it may be used for tiles, tubs, sinks, and porcelain. And for all around the house, it may be used on floors, garbage cans, in the basement, and in the garage.

Can I use this inside my refrigerator?
ANSWER: Lysol may be used on the inside of a refrigerator. However, you must remove all food, and rinse well after using the product.

Can I use this to kill mold and mildew?
Yes. Lysol controls the growth of mold and mildew. It kills the mold, but removal of the stain associated with mold and mildew can sometimes be tough.

Can I use this to scrub the uncontrollable black from the surface of my daughter, to make her less Negro and somehow less embarrassing to me? She's like the hour after midnight, that chile is.

Why, yes. Begin with one Sears gray swirled dinette set chair, screeching across the hardwood on spindly steel legs. Place the offending child on the ruptured plastic of the seat. Demand that she bend her neck to grant you access to the damaged area. You know, of course, that black begins at the back of the neck. Grab a kitchen towel, a washcloth, or a sponge, and soak with undiluted Lysol concentrate.

Ignoring the howls of the impossibly Negro child, scrub vigorously until the offending black surrenders. There may be inflammation, a painful rebellion of skin, slight bleeding. This is simply the first step to righteousness. The child must be punished for her lack of silky tresses, her broad sinful nose, that dark Negroid blanket she wears. Layers of her must disappear.

PRECAUTIONARY STATEMENTS. DANGER: CORROSIVE TO EYES AND SKIN. HARMFUL IF SWALLOWED. Causes eye and skin damage. Do not get in eyes or on skin. Wear protective eyewear and rubber gloves when handling.

Woman, your mission is beyond this. You must clean the child, burn the Southern sun from her. If she squirms from the hurting, demand that she hold on to the sides of the chair. Soak towel or sponge with our patented holy water. Repeat application.

I have tried to understand PRECAUTIONARY STATEMENTS my mother DANGER: her hatred of this CORROSIVE TO EYES AND SKIN of the me that wears this HARMFUL IF SWALLOWED the monster she had CAUSES EYE AND SKIN DAMAGE the monster she wanted DO NOT GET IN EYES OR ON SKIN

Mama, can't you read it? You want me to read it to you? I can't help being my color! I am black, I am not dirty. I am black, I am not dirty, I am black, I am. Not. Dirty. What you have birthed upon me will not come off. My hair is black crinkled steel, too short to stay plaited. My ass is wide and will get wider. You can pinch my nose, but it will remain a landscape. You cannot reverse me. What is filthy to you will never be cleansed. There is only one thing you can

change

I am not dirty, I am black. I am not dirty, I am black, I am not black, I am dirty. I am dirty black, not black. I am black and dirty. Dirt is black. Black is dirty. You convinced me that I am what is wrong in this world.

Scrub me right.
Bleed me lighter.

What is the difference between disinfection and sanitization? Why are there two different usage directions far each?

ANSWER: According to the Environmental Protection Agency, "disinfection" is killing more than 99.99% of germs on hard, nonporous surfaces in ten minutes, and may pertain to a number of different types of bacteria, viruses, and fungi. The EPA defines "sanitization" as killing 99.9% of bacteria in five minutes or less.

Lysol products achieve sanitization in 30 seconds.

29. 28. 27. 26. 25. 24. 23. 22. 21. 20. 19. 18. 17. 16. 15. 14. 13. 12. 11. 10. 9. 8. 7. 6. 5. 4. 3. 2....

Done.

Because

we sipped blood siphoned from grocery store grapes
Because matrons squinted at the dim crackling pages of hymnals
Because we obediently warbled exactly what we found there
Because spurting prompt hallelujahs was serious business
Because my mother's gilded tooth flashed when she begged
Because on Sundays we presented God with several options
Because Rev. Thomas's sick ankles were stiff and blue with fluid
Because his spat truths were mangled by bad tooth and spittle
Because he made seventy-two years move like some golden engine
Because Tony the choir director was, how you say it, a sissy
Because that old organ wailed like the B-side of a backslap
Because the pocked wooden floor left language on our knees
Because the rafters grew slimy with wailing, because, well,
because Judas, a pimp in blacklight, was smirking at Jesus again
Because somebody definitely acted up and conjured Mississippi
Because salt pork flailed in a skillet in the basement kitchen
Because Lawd knows we were all gon' be crazy hungry
Because the Holy Ghost was dawdling in the men's room
Because He had scanned the crowd and wasn't crazy about His odds
Because the grandbabies of freed slaves shimmied in their seats
Because every upright elder in the front row blathered with fever
Because crosses, unblessed with bodies, were everywhere
Because every one of those wooden T's bellowed out loud
Because, just like last time, the fun-word-of-the-day was *sacrifice*
Because that sissy popped like a tear dripped on a red stovetop
Because he flowed our whole upturned voice from his fingers
Because worshippers with straightened hair wept slivers of Delta
Because we were a tangled mess of sanctified thighs and tongues
Because several instigators whispered *Just felt the Ghost come in*
Because Annie Pearl Smith's dazzled eyes got all-the-way wide
Because her numbed and hard-girdled waistline twisted in bliss
Because thick bodies hit the floor hard, squalling, convulsing,

Because prim ushers dug white-gloved fingers into her forearms
Because I had to gaze into the peppermint of my mother's wail
Because I questioned what soft, holy monster writhed inside her
Because I had once again been spared the slick sleight hand
of the devious divinity, because that twirling sissy and I
loved wrong and were loved wrong, because when Tony sniffed
haughty at the thrashing, collapsing congregation and whipped the choir
in the direction of flame, I felt the organ's bright asking drip like fuel
into the blood feeding my little hip. So I struck the match.

To Keep from Saying *Dead*

For Gwendolyn Brooks

Winter, with its numbing gusts and giddy twists of ice,
is gone now. It's time for warmth again.
So where is Gwendolyn Brooks?
Its huge shoulders slumped, Chicago craves her hobble,
turns pissed and gray, undusts her name.

To know her,
you need to ride her city's wide watery hips,
you need to inhale an obscene sausage
smothered in gold slipping onions
while standing on a chaotic streetcross
where any jazz could be yours.
Walk the hurting fields of the West Side,
our slice of city burned to bones in '68—

Goldblatt's, the colored Bloomingdale's, gone.

Lerners, where we learned pinafore, gone.

No more havens for layaway, no more places
to plop down a dollar a week for P.F. Flyers
or wool jumpers with seams glued shut.
The meat market with its bloody sawdust, torched,
its Jewish proprietors now crisping languid
under Florida sun. And flap-jowled Mayor Daley,
our big benevolent murderous daddy,
gifted us with high-rise castles crafted of dirty dollars,
battered cans of bumpy milk, free cheese.

To know Gwen, you need to know the Alex,
the only movie theater West, where frisky rats
big as toddlers poked slow noses into your popcorn,

then locked red round eyes on Cleopatra Jones
and sat, confident and transfixed.

After the movies and any street corner's fried lunch,
we'd head to "the store in back of that fat man's house"
to surrender hoarded quarters for the latest 45,
stripped licorice in black or red,
pork rinds, Boston Baked Beans,
or fat sour pickles floating in a jar in the corner.
The fat man's wife, Miss Caroline,
plunged her hammy forearm into the brine,
pulled out the exact pickle you pointed to
and shoved it deep into a single-ply paper bag.
Only the truly Negro would then poke
a peppermint stick down the center of that pickle
and slurp the dizzy of salt and sugar.
We gnawed rock-stiff candy dots off paper columns,
suffered Lemonheads and Red Hots,
pushed neon sweatsocks down on Vaselined calves,
and my Lord, we learned to switch. For a dime,
the fat man would warm up the record player,
click reject and give us a hit of Ms. Fontella Bass's
heartbroke heart clamoring for rescue,
or Ruby Andrews steady wailing in a woman way.

There were so many millions of each one of us,
ashy goddesses walking the wild West,
strutting past sloped storefronts where brown meat
and hog heads crowded the windows,
past shuttered groceries, and gas stations
with pump boys eyeing our new undulating asses,
past fashion palaces where almost no money
satisfied our yearning for hollow glamour
with cheap threads already unraveling.

Observe the kick-ass angle of our crowns.
Chicago girls just keep coming back.
They don't hear you,
they don't see you,
they ain't never really needed you.
They got the Holy Ghost and Garfield Park,
on one city block, they got a hundred ways to buy chicken,
they jump rope nasty and barefoot in the dirt,
they got the *ooh achie koo,*
the pink plastic clothesline underhand,
they got the slip bone. They got the Gwen in them.

Any jazz could be ours, and her jazz was.
Unflinching in riotous headwrap
and thick, two-shades-too stockings,
she penned the soundtrack of we because she knew,
because she was skinny early church and not bending,
because no man could ever hold her the way hurt did,
because she could peer at you over those Coke-bottle specs,
fast gal, and turn the sorry sight of you into her next poem.

Each year she stays gone, we colored girls aimlessly bop
and search dangerous places for music.
Chicago bows its huge head, grudgingly accepts spring.

God, if there is a You, there must surely still be a her.
Stop the relentless seasons. Show us Your face,
explain Your skewed timing,
Your wacky choice of angels.

13 Ways of Looking at 13

1.

You touch your forefinger to the fat clots in the blood,
then lift its iron stench to look close, searching the globs
of black scarlet for the dimming swirl of dead children.
You thread one thick pad's cottony tail, then the other,
through the little steel guides of the belt. You stand and lift
the contraption, press your thighs close to adjust the bulk,
then bend to pull up coarse white cotton panties bleached blue,
and just to be safe, you pin the bottom of the pad
to the shredding crotch of the Carter's. And then you spritz
the guilty air with the cloying kiss of FDS.
It's time to begin the game of justifying ache,
time to name the mystery prickling riding your skin.
You're convinced the boys can smell you, and they can, they can.

2.

Right now, this Tuesday in July, nothing's headier
than the words *Sheen! Manageable! Bounce!* Squinting into
the smeared mirror, you search your ghetto-ripe head for them,
you probe with greased fingers, spreading paths in the chaos
wide enough for the advertised glimmer to escape,
but your snarls hold tight to their woven dry confounding.
Fevered strands snap under the drag of the wiry brush
and order unfurls, while down the hall mama rotates
the hot comb in a bleary blaze, smacks her joyful gum.
Still, TV bellows its promise. You witness the pink
snap of the perfect neck, hear the impossible vow—
Shampoo with this! *Sheen! Bounce!* Her cornsilk head is gospel,
it's true. *C'mon chile!* Even mama's summoning burns.

3.

Ms. Stein scribbled a word on the blackboard, said *Who can
pronounce this?* and the word was *anemone* and from
that moment you first felt the clutter of possible
in your mouth, from the time you stumbled through the rhythm
and she slow-smiled, you suddenly knew you had the right
to be explosive, to sling syllables through back doors,
to make up your own damned words just when you needed them.
All that day, sweet *anemone* tangled in your teeth,
spurted sugar tongue, led you to the dictionary
where you were assured that it existed, to the cave
of the bathroom where you warbled it in bounce echo,
and, finally convinced you owned that teeny gospel,
you wrote it again and again and again and a—.

4.

Trying hard to turn hips to slivers, sway to stutter,
you walk past the Sinclair station where lanky boys, dust
in their hair, dressed in their uniforms of oil and thud,
rename you *pussy* with their eyes. They bring sounds shudder
and blue from their throats just for you, serve up the ancient
sonata of skin drum and conch shell, sing suggesting woos
of AM radio, boom, boom, *How you gon' just walk
on by like that?* and suddenly you know why you are
stitched so tight, crammed like a flash bomb into pinafore,
obeying Mama's instructions to be a baby
as long as you can. Because it's a man's world and James
Brown is gasoline, the other side of slow zippers.
He is all of it, the pump, pump, the growled *please please please.*

5.

You try to keep your hands off your face, but the white-capped
pimples might harbor evil. It looks like something cursed

is trying to escape your cheeks, your whole soul could be
involved. So you pinch, squeeze, and pop, let the smelly snow
splash the mirror, slather your fresh-scarred landscape with creams
that clog and strangle. At night, you look just like someone
obsessed with the moon, its gruff superstitions, its lies.
Your skin is a patchwork of wishing. You scrub and dab
and mask and surround, you bombard, spritz, and peel, rubbing
alcohol, flesh-toned Clearasil that pinkens and cakes
while new dirtworms shimmy beneath the pummeled surface
of you. Every time you touch your face, you leave a scar.
Hey, you. Every time you touch your face, you leave a scar.

6.

You want it all: chicken wings with bubbled skin fried tight,
salmon cakes in syrup, the most improbable parts
of swine, oily sardines on saltines splashed in red spark,
chitlins nurtured and scraped in Saturday assembly,
buttered piecrusts stuffed with sweet potatoes and sugar,
gray cheese conjured from the heads of hogs. All that Dixie
dirt binds, punches your insides flat, reteaches the blind
beat of your days. Like Mama and her mother before
her, you pulse on what is thrown away—gray hog guts stewed
improbable and limp, scrawny chicken necks merely
whispering meat. You will live beyond the naysayers,
your rebellious heart constructed of lard and salt, your
life labored but long. You are built of what should kill you.

7.

Always treat white folks right, your mama's mantra again
and yet again, *because they give you things.* Like credit,
compliments, passing grades, government jobs, direction,
extra S&H stamps, produce painted to look fresh,
a religion. When the insurance man came, she snapped
herself alive, hurriedly rearranged her warm bulk. He

was balding badly, thatches of brown on a scabbed globe.
Just sign here, he hissed, staring crave into her huge breasts,
pocketing the death cash, money she would pay and pay
and never see again. *C'mere girl, say hello to*
Mister Fred. She had taught you to bow. She taught him
to ignore the gesture, to lock his watering eyes
to yours and lick his dry lips with a thick, coated tongue.

8.

In the bathroom of the what-not joint on the way to
school, you get rid of the starch and billowed lace, barrettes
taming unraveling braids, white kneesocks and sensible
hues. From a plastic bag, you take out electric blue
eye shadow, platforms with silver-glittered heels, neon
fishnets, and a blouse that doesn't so much button as
snap shut. The transformation takes five minutes, and you
emerge feeling like a budding lady but looking,
in retrospect, like a blind streetwalker bursting from
a cocoon. This is what television does, turns your
mother into clueless backdrop, fills your pressed head with
the probability of thrum. Your body becomes
just not yours anymore. It's a dumb little marquee.

9.

With your bedroom door closed, you are skyscraper bouffant,
peach foundation, eyelashes like upturned claws. You are
exuding ice, pinched all over by earrings, you are
too much of woman for this room. The audience has
one chest, a single shared chance to gasp. They shudder, heave,
waiting for you to open your mouth and break their hearts.
Taking the stage, you become an S, pour ache into your
hip swings, *tsk tsk* as the front row collapses. Damn, they
want you. You lift the microphone, something illegal
comes out of you, a sound like titties and oil. Mama

flings the door open with a church version of your name.
Then you are pimpled, sexless, ashed and doubledutch knees.
You are spindles. You are singing into a hairbrush.

10.

This is what everyone else is doing: skating in
soul circles, skinning shins, tongue-kissing in the coatroom,
skimming alleys for Chicago rats, failing English, math,
crushing curfew, lying about yesterday and age,
slipping Woolworth's bounty into an inside pocket,
sprouting breasts. Here is what everyone else is doing:
sampling the hotness of hootch, grinding under blue light,
getting turned around in the subway, flinging all them
curse words, inhaling a quick supper before supper
fried up in hot Crisco and granulated sugar,
sneaking out through open windows when the night goes dark,
calling mamas bitches under their breath, staying up
till dawn to see what hides. What *you* are doing: Reading.

11.

You are never too old. And you are never too world,
too almost grown, you are never correct, no matter
how many times you are corrected. It is never
too late, never too early to be told to cross the
street to the place where the wild stuff is, to suffer her
instructions: *No, not that little switch, get the big one,*
the one that makes that good whipping sound when the breeze blows,
and you are never too fast crossing the boulevard
to bring it back while winged sedans carve jazz on your path.
You climb the stairs, she screams *Get up here!* The door to where
you live with her flies open. She snatches the thorned branch,
whips it a hundred times across the backs of your legs.
You want her to die. Not once, no. Many times. Gently.

12.

That boy does not see you. He sees through you, past your tone
of undecided earth. You are the exact shade of
the failed paper bag test, the Aunt Esther, you are hair
forever turning back in the direction from which
it came. You are clacking knees and nails bitten to blood.
Stumbling forth in black, Jesus-prescribed shoes, you have no
knowledge of his knowledge of hip sling and thrust. That boy
does not see you. So squeeze your eyes shut and imagine
your mouth touching the swell of his forearm. Imagine
just your name's first syllable in the sugared well of
his throat. Dream of all the ways he is not walking past
you again, turning his eyes to the place where you are,
where you're standing, where you shake, where you pray, where you aren't.

13.

You're almost fourteen. And you think you're ready to push
beyond the brutal wisdoms of the one and the three,
but some nagging crave in you doesn't want to let go.
You suspect that you will never be this unfinished,
all Hail Mary and precipice, stuttering sashay,
fuses in your swollen chest suddenly lit, spitting,
and you'll need to give your hips a name for what they did
while you weren't there. You'll miss the pervasive fever that
signals bloom, the sore lessons of jumprope in your calves.
This is the last year your father is allowed to touch
you. Sighing, you push Barbie's perfect body through the
thick dust of a top shelf. There her prideful heart thunders.
She has hardened you well. She has taught you everything.

Hip-Hop Ghazal

Gotta love us brown girls, munching on fat, swinging blue hips,
decked out in shells and splashes, Lawdie, bringing them woo hips.

As the jukebox teases, watch my sistas throat the heartbreak,
inhaling bass line, cracking backbone and singing thru hips.

Like something boneless, we glide silent, seeping 'tween floorboards,
wrapping around the hims, and *ooh wee*, clinging like glue hips.

Engines, grinding, rotating, smokin', gotta pull back some.
Natural minds are lost at the mere sight of swinging true hips.

Gotta love us girls, just struttin' down Chicago streets
killing the menfolk with a dose of that stinging view. Hips.

Crying 'bout getting old—Patricia, you need to get up off
what God gave you. Say a prayer and start slinging. Cue hips.

Thief of Tongues

1.

My mother is learning English.
Pulling rubbery cinnamon-tinged hose to a roll beneath
her knees, sporting one swirling Baptist ski slope of a hat,
she rides the rattling elevated to a Windy City spire
and pulls back her gulp as the elevator hurtles heaven.
Then she's stiffly seated at a scarred oak table
across from a white, government-sanctioned savior
who has dedicated eight hours a week to straightening
afflicted black tongues. She guides my mother
patiently through lazy *ings* and *ers*, slowly scraping
her throat clean of the moist and raging infection
of Aliceville, Alabama. There are barely muttered
apologies for colored sounds. There is much beginning again.

I want to talk right before I die.
Want to stop saying "ain't" and "I done been"
like I ain't got no sense. I'm a grown woman.
I done lived too long to be stupid,
acting like I just got off the boat.

My mother
has never been
on a boat.

But fifty years ago, merely a million of her,
clutching strapped cases. *Jet's* Emmett Till issue,
and thick-peppered chicken wings in waxed bags,
stepped off hot rumbling buses at Northern depots
in Detroit, in Philly, in the bricked cornfield of Chicago.
Brushing stubborn scarlet dust from their shoes,
they said *We North now*, slinging it in backdoor syllable,

as if those three words were vessels big enough
to hold country folks' overwrought ideas of light.

2.

Back then, my mother thought it a modern miracle,
this new living in a box stacked upon other boxes,
where every flat surface reeked of Lysol and effort,
and chubby roaches, cross-eyed with Raid,
dragged themselves across freshly washed dishes
and dropped dizzy from the ceiling into our Murphy beds,
our washtubs, our open steaming pots of collards.

Of course, there was a factory just two bus rides close,
a job that didn't involve white babies or bluing laundry,
where she worked in tense line with other dreamers:
Repeatedly. Repeatedly. Repeatedly. Repeatedly,
all those oily hotcombed heads drooping, no talking
as scarred brown hands romanced machines, just
the sound of doin' it right, and Juicy Fruit crackling.
A mere mindset away, there had to be a corner tavern
where dead bluesmen begged second chances from the juke,
and where my mama, perched man-wary on a comfortable stool
by the door, could look like a Christian who was just leaving.

And on Sunday, at Pilgrim Rest Missionary Baptist Church,
she would pull on the pure white gloves of service
and wail to the rafters when the Holy Ghost's hot hand
grew itchy and insistent at the small of her back.
She was His child, finally loosed of that damnable Delta,
building herself anew in this land of sidewalks,
blue jukes, and sizzling fried perch in virgin-white boxes
See her: all nap burned from her crown, one gold tooth
winking, soft hair riding her lip, blouses starched hard,
orlon sweaters with smatterings of stitched roses,
A-line skirts the color of unleashed winter.

3.

My mother's voice is like homemade cornbread,
slathered with butter, full of places for heat to hide.
When she is pissed, it punches straight out
and clears the room. When she is scared,
it turns practical, matter-of-fact, like when she called
to say
They found your daddy this morning,
somebody shot him, he dead.
He ain't come to work this morning, I knowed
something was wrong.
When mama talks, the Southern swing of it
is wild with unexpected blooms,
like the fields she never told me about in Alabama.
Her rap is peppered with *ain't gots* and *I done beens*
and *he be's* just like mine is when I'm color among color.
During worship, when talk becomes song, her voice collapses
and loses all acquaintance with key, so of course,
it's my mother's fractured alto wailing above everyone—
uncaged, unapologetic and creaking toward heaven.

Now she wants to sound proper when she gets there.
A woman got some sense and future need to upright herself,
talk English instead of talking wrong.

It's strange to hear the precise rote of Annie Pearl's new mouth.
She slips sometimes, but is proud when she remembers
to bite down on dirt-crafted contractions and double negatives.

Sometimes I wonder whatever happened to the warm expanse
of the red-dust woman, who arrived with a little sin
and all the good wrong words. I dream her breathless,
maybe leaning forward a little in her seat on the Greyhound.
I ain't never seen, she begins, grinning through the grime
at Chicago, city of huge shoulders, thief of tongues.

Motown Crown

The Temps, all swerve and pivot, conjured schemes
that had us skipping school, made us forget
how mamas schooled us hard against the threat
of five-part harmony and sharkskin seams.
We spent our school days balanced on the beams
of moon we wished upon, the needled jet-
black 45s that spun and hadn't yet
become the dizzy spinning of our dreams.
Sugar pie, honey bunch . . . oh, you
loved our tangled hair and rusty knees.
Marvin Gaye slowed down while we gave chase
then wowed us with his skinny hips, on cue.
We hungered for the anguished screech of *Please*
from soulful throats. Relentless. Booming bass.

From soulful throats, relentless booming bass
softened with the turn of Smokey's key.
His languid, liquid, luscious, aching plea
for bodies we didn't have yet made a case
for lying to ourselves. He would embrace
our naps and raging pimples. We could see
his croon inside our clothes. His pedigree
of milky flawless skin meant we'd replace
our *daddies* with his fine and lanky frame.
I did you wrong, my heart went out to play
he serenaded, filling up the space
that separated Smoke from certain flame.
Couldn't comprehend the drug of him, his sway,
silk where his throat should be. He growled such grace.

Silk where his throat should be, and growling grace,
Little Stevie made us wonder why

we even *needed* sight. His rhythm eye
could see us click our hips and pump in place
whenever he cut loose. Ooh, we'd unlace
our Converse All-Stars, yeah, we wondered why
we couldn't get down *without* our shoes. We'd try
to dance and keep up with his funky pace
of hiss and howl and hum, and then he'd slow
to twist our hearts until he heard them crack,
ignoring lonesome leaking from the seams.
The rockin' blind boy couldn't help but show
us light. We wailed his every soulful track
through open windows, 'neath the door—pipe dreams.

Through open windows, 'neath the doors, pipe dreams
served up bone, bouffant, the serpentine
and bug-eyed Lady D, the boisterous queen
of overdone, her body build from beams
of awkward light. Her slithering extremes
just made us feel so small. Insanely lean,
everywhere she stepped she caused a scene.
We craved her wigs and waist and crafted schemes
that would ensure our hips would soon be thin,
that we'd hear symphonies, wouldn't hurry love,
'cause Diana said *Make sure it gleams*
no matter what it is. Her different spin,
a voice like sugar air, no inkling of
a soul beneath the vinyl. The Supremes.

That soul beneath the vinyl, the Supremes
knew nothing of it. They were breathy sighs
and flowing hips, soul music's booby prize.
But Mary Wells, so drained of self-esteem,
was a pudgy, barstool-ridin' bucktoothed dream
who none of us would dare to idolize

out loud. She had our nightmares memorized
and like or like it not, she wailed our theme
while her too-blackness made us ill at ease
and we smeared Artra on to reach for white.
When Mary's *My Guy* blared, we didn't think race,
'cause there was all that romance, and the keys
that Motown held. Unlocked, we'd soon ignite.
We stockpiled extra sequins, just in case.

We stockpiled extra sequins, just in case
the Marvelettes pronounced we'd benefit
from little dabs of shine. If we could get
inside their swirl, a kinda naughty place,
we knew that all the boys would have to brace
themselves against our heat, much too legit
to dress up as some other thing. We split
our blue jeans trying to match their pace.
And soon our breasts began to pop, we spoke
in bluer tones, and Berry Gordy looked
and licked his lips. Our only saving grace?
The luscious, liquid languid tone of Smoke,
the soundtrack while our A-cup bras unhooked.
Our sudden Negro hips required more space.

Our sudden Negro hips required more space,
but we pretended not to feel that spill
that changed the way we walked. And yes, we still
felt nappy, awkward, strangely out of place
while Motown crammed our eager hearts with lace
and storylines. Romance was all uphill.
No push, no prod, no bitter magic pill
could lift us to its light. And not a trace
of prizes they said we'd already won.
As mamas called on Jesus, shook their heads

and mourned our Delta names, we didn't deem
to care. Religion—there was only one.
We took transistor preachers to our beds
and Smokey sang a lyric dripping cream.

While Smokey sang a lyric dripping cream,
Levi tried to woo us with his growl:
Can't help myself. Admitted with a scowl,
this bit of weakness was a clever scheme
to keep us screaming, front row, under gleam
of lights, beside the speakers' blasting vowels.
We rocked and steamed. Levi, on the prowl,
glowed black, a savior in the stage light's beam.
But then the stage light dimmed, and there we were
in bodies primed—for what we didn't know.
We sang off-key while skipping home alone.
Deceptions that you sing to tend to blur
and disappear in dance, why is that so?
Ask any colored girl and she will moan.

Ask any colored girl and she will moan
an answer with a downbeat and a sleek
five-part croon. She's dazzled, and she'll shriek
what she's been taught. She won't long be alone,
or crazed with wanting more. One day she'll own
that quiet heart that Motown taught to speak,
she'll know that being the same makes her unique.
She'll worship at the god of microphone
until the bass line booms, until some old
Temptation leers and says *I'll take you home
and heal you in the way the music vowed.*
She's mesmerized—his moves, that tooth of gold.
She dances to the drumbeat of his poem,
remembering how. Love had lied so loud.

Remembering how love had lied so loud,
we tangled in the rhythms that we chose.
Seduced by thump and sequins, heaven knows
we tried to live our hopeful lives unbowed,
but bending led to break. We were so proud
to mirror every lyric. Radios
spit beg and mend, and sturdy stereos
told us what we were and weren't allowed.
Our daddies sweat in factories while we
found other daddies under limelight's glow.
Desperate, we begged them to illuminate
the glitter lives they used to guarantee
would save us. But instead, the crippling blow.
We whimpered while the downbeat dangled bait.

We whimpered while the downbeat dangled bait,
we leapt and swallowed all the music said
while Smokey laughed and Marvin fell and bled.
Their sinning slapped us hard and slapped us straight,
and even then, we listened for the great
announcement of the drum, for tune to spread,
a Marvelette to pick up on the thread.
But as we know by now, it's much too late
to reconsider love, or claw our way
through all the glow they tossed to slow our roll.
What we know now we should have always known.
When Smokey winked at us and whispered *They
don't love you like I do*, he snagged our soul.
We wound up doing the slow drag, all alone.

They made us do the slow drag, all alone.
They made us kiss our mirrors, deal with heat
and hips we couldn't control. They danced deceit
and we did too, addicted to the drone

of revelation and the verses thrown
our way: *Oh, love will rock your world. The sweet*
sweet fairy tale we spin will certainly beat
the real thing any day. Oh, yes we own
you now. We sang you pliable and clue-
less, waiting, waiting, oh the dream you'll hug
one day, the boy who craves you right out loud
in front of everyone. But we told you,
we know we did, we preached it with a shrug—
less than perfect love was not allowed.

Less than perfect love was not allowed.
Temptations begged as if their every sway
depended on you coming home to stay.
Diana whispered air, aloof and proud
to be the perfect girl beneath a shroud
of glitter and a fright she held at bay.
And Michael Jackson, flailing in the fray
of daddy love, succumbed to every crowd.
What would we have done if not for them,
wooing us with roses carved of sound
and hiding muck we're born to navigate?
Little did we know that they'd condemn
us to live so tethered to the ground
while every song they sang told us to wait.

Every song they sang told us to wait
and wait we did, our gangly heartbeats stunned
and holding place. Already so outgunned,
we little girls obeyed. And now it's late,
and CDs spinning just intimidate.
The songs all say, *Just look at what you've done,*
you've wished through your whole life. And one by one
your trusting sisters realize they don't rate.

So now, at fifty-plus, I turn around
and see the glitter drifting in my wake
and mingling with the dirt. My dingy dreams
are shoved high on the shelf. They've wrapped and bound
so I can't see and contemplate the ache.
The Temps, all swirl and pivot, conjured schemes.

The Temps, all swirl and pivot, conjured schemes
from soulful throats, relentless booming bass,
then silk where throats should be. Much growling grace
from open window, 'neath the door, pipe dreams—
that soul beneath the vinyl. The Supremes
used to stockpile extra sequins just in case
Diana's Negro hips required more space,
while Smokey penned a lyric dripping cream.
Ask any colored girl, and she will moan,
remembering how love had lied so loud.
I whimpered while the downbeat dangled bait
and taught myself to slow drag, all alone.
Less than perfect love was not allowed
and every song they sang told me to wait.

Incendiary Art, 2017

People don't recognize this country. It is war-thirsty, swaggering, oblivious, scornful of the other, villainous, bloated. The poet remembers all of the country. How it growled at her childhood. How it sent her mama downtown for English lessons from a white woman. How it drowned that boy from Chicago. How it taught her daddy the corners of factory. How it killed and kills—soldiers, numbers-runners, m'dears, pump jockeys, auto workers, druggies, sex workers, the fresh-born. How faultlessly it draws chalk outlines. How it gloats when something burns. Now the poet knows sestinas, caesuras, sonnets, enjambments, and the muscle of the line break. Now she can layer music over hurting. Now she can say the quiet things out loud.

That Chile Emmett in That Casket

Photo, Jet *magazine, Sept. 15, 1955*

Sometimes the page was tacked, flush against plaster with a pearl hatpin,
or jammed into a dime-store frame with a glowing Jesus. In some kingly

front rooms, its place was in the shadowbox, propped on one ripped edge,
or laid curly-cornered on the coffee table, smudged and eaten sheer

with the pass-around. In the kitchen, it was blurred by stew smoke
or pot liquor–blotched until somebody got smart enough to Scotch tape

it to door of the humming fridge, and the boy without eyes kept staring.
Mamas did the slow fold before wedging it into their flowered plastic

coin purses, daddies found a sacred place in pleather wallets right next
to the thought of cash. And at least once every week, usually on Sunday

after church or when you dared think you didn't have to speak proper
to that old white lady who answered the phone at your daddy's job,

or when, as Mama said, you *showed your ass* by sassin' or backtalking,
the page would be pulled down, pulled out, unfolded, smoothed flat,

and you had to look. *Look, girl.* And they made sure you kept looking
while your daddy shook his head, mumbling *This why you got to act*

right 'round white folk, then dropped his smoke-threaded gaze to whisper
Lord, they kilt that chile more than one time. Mama held on to your eyes—

See what happen when you don't be careful? She meant white men could
turn you into a stupid reason for a dress, that your last face would be silt,

stunned in its skid and worshipped, your right eye reborn in the cave
of your mouth. *Look!* she screeched. You did. But then you remembered

there weren't any pictures of *you* in the house, pinned high on the wall,
folded up tight up against the Lord, toted like talisman in wallet or purse.

You'd searched, woe climbing like river in your chest. But there were
no pictures of you anywhere. You sparked no moral. You were alive.

Incendiary Art

The city's streets are densely shelved with rows
of salt and packaged hair. Intent on air,
the funk of crave and function comes to blows

with any smell that isn't oil—the blare
of storefront chicken settles on the skin
and mango spritzing drips from razored hair.

The corner chefs cube pork, decide again
on cayenne, fry in grease that's glopped with dust.
The sizzle of the feast adds to the din

of children strutting slant, their wanderlust
and cussing, plus the loud and tactless hiss
of dogged hustlers bellowing past gusts

of peppered breeze, that fatty, fragrant bliss
in skillets. All our rampant hunger tricks
us into thinking we can dare dismiss

the thing men do to boulevards, the wicks
their bodies be. A city, strapped for art,
delights in torching them—at first for kicks,

to waltz to whirling sparks, but soon those hearts
thud thinner, whittled by the chomp of heat.
Outlined in chalk, men blacken, curl apart.

Their blindly rising fume is bittersweet,
although reversals in the air could fool
us into thinking they weren't meant as meat.

Our sons don't burn their cities as a rule,
born, as they are, up to their necks in fuel.

Emmett Till: Choose Your Own Adventure

Mamie Till had hoped to take her son Emmett on a vacation to visit relatives in Nebraska. Instead, he begged her to let him visit his cousins in Mississippi.

Turn to page 194 if Emmett travels to Nebraska instead of Mississippi.

Incessantly, his mother quotes her God
while wrestling with the Plymouth's snarl and clunk.
The country's hellish breadth, its dank facade
conspire to make him blue and snappish, drunk
with dozing. Windows blur with foliage
and sweep. At roadside stops, the poison-eyed
and devilish slurp their tepid Cokes and gauge
his spine. Pretending he's preoccupied
with being from a place they can't decode
and knowing what they don't, he steels his back
against their hawk and spittle 'til the road
and Mamie call. To swagger past the pack,
he's learned to turn their threats to anecdote
and chuckle at the squeeze that begs for throat.

Incendiary Art: Birmingham, 1963

For avery r. young

Baby girls boom. Baby girls blow
and burn, skin balloons, booms.
Baby girls burn, boom. The Lord
dangles, festive and helpless.
Hymnals blacken while brown
baby girls pucker, leak. Blood jells,
muddles pigtail, makes lace stiff.
Baby girls blacken, crackle
in the vague direction of His hands
nailed still. Baby brown girl bodies
gap wide, wider, char and shut.

Emmett Till: Choose Your Own Adventure

Mamie Till insisted on an open casket so that the world could see her son's mutilated body. More than 50,000 people filed past during his funeral. Many screamed or fainted.

Turn to page 196 if Emmett's casket was closed instead.

We're curious, but his imploded eye,
the bullet's only door, would be the thing
we wouldn't want to see. We justify
his childish glint, and sigh, imagining
the knotted tie, the scissored naps, those cheeks
in rakish bloom, perhaps a scrape or two
beneath his laundered shirt. The mourners' shrieks
are tangled with an organ's point of view,
and someone moans Mahalia. Mamie's fanned
and comforted, her gorgeous fallen son
a horrid hidden rot. Her tiny hand
starts crushing roses—one by one by one
she wrecks the casket's spray. It's how she mourns—
a mother, still, despite the roar of thorns.

Hey, who you got in here?

My boy. Who you come to see?

My son. How old your boy?

21. How old your son?

19.

I seen you here a lot. Where you live?

West Side, over by Garfield Park. Where you live?

New York. Well, close to New York anyway.

And you come all this way?

Sho' don't feel like it.

Hot in here, ain't it?

Yep. Hot in here. Always is.

Wonder if the folks locked up is this hot all the time.

Hell, they in jail. Ain't sposed to be comfortable.

Hard coming out here.

Yeah. Hard.

I like your hair. Been thinking about getting those braids.

Take a long time.

I know. Three hours?

Girl, more than that. Your boy done cut all his hair off yet?

Uh-huh. Bald as the day he hit this world.

First thing they do, shave that head. Wonder why.

Ain't much else to do, I guess.

I guess.

They need to get some air in here. What they mad at *us* for?

Chile, you right. We ain't done nothing.

Always so damn hot.

Why your boy here? What he do? You don't have to—

Chile, I don't care. He in here for being stupid. Lord knows I—

Tried, I know.

Maybe he learn something in here. I tried to warn his black ass.

But they don't listen. Think they grown 'fore they grown.

I hear that. Shame to see so many of them in here though.

I know. Feel like we in another country.

I get tired of coming out here.

Me too.

Don't nothing change. Always so hot.

Girl, turn around, lemme see. I sho' like those braids. Real nice in back.

Thanks.

I need to get rid of this perm. Hell, gon' sweat it out in here.

Gotta remember to ask that boy if it's this hot—

Um-uh, all the time.

How long he gon' be in here?

End of next year. But he got another think coming if he think he—

Trying to come lay up in your house, huh?

Oh, he *think* he is. How long your chile here?

Another two years.

That's a long time.

Pass fast when you get old as me.

What you, 35? 36?

Almost.

Chile, I'm 40. Too old for this shit.

I can't get over how hot it is. I'm gon' say something.

Me too, let's say something. It ain't like *we* in jail.

Look. Look over there. You know that sister? She here a lot.

Uh-huh. Hey.

Hey.

Hey. How you doing? Figured we might as well speak.

We see you here a lot. Who you come to see?

My son. Who y'all come to see?

We got boys in here too. How old your boy?

He 20.

Damn, it's hot in here.

Girl, we was just saying.

We gon' say something about it this time. Don't make no damn sense.

Yeah, we gon' say something.

It's like they tryin' to—

Chile, I know. Kill us in here.

Incendiary Art: Los Angeles, 1992

Heard on the day they found Rodney King face down at the
bottom of a swimming pool: *Nigger could take an ass whuppin',
but he couldn't swim! Ain't that something?*

1

You can name yourself a man, walk taut and tall and will your voice
to stomp, but still be upended by demons, ain't that something?

Tiny bones in your cheek, smashed, went fluid. Dumbstruck, you were pissed
by the sour taint of your sad, sputtered imploring. That something

you thought God was supposed to do for you wasn't this—your neck
slamming shut for its own safety. You were a man. That, something

else, and something other were whupped straight out of you that evening,
whizzing cudgels answered and answered when you swore that something

your swagger said that morning should still apply. All you wanted
was to find your feet and stand up. And you prayed that something

curling orange on the horizon would be fit to breathe, because
you'd rather burn than die cowering, clobbered flat, a numb king.

2

It's no surprise that you coveted the water—born, as you
were, up to your neck in fuel. We wished we could undo that night—

your ragged floodlit flail and swell, bulge of bone, all those scars of
incendiary art. Roadside Jesus, all you knew that night

were ways to turn and turn the other mangled cheek. You gave them
no choice but to heft the cross. You were pummeled blood-blue that night,

then looped and relooped for moral while brick buildings took on ghost,
and mamas howled and clawed their babies' naps for ash. You, that night,

were wick, and your city was a heinous grin, a hard-struck match.
It took all those years to shush your fume. Yes, you lived through that night,

but dreamed of plunging into a blameless cool, your hot head sick
with steam, a cheap tarnished crown bobbing—at last—into the light.

Black, Poured Directly into the Wound

A double golden shovel

Prairie winds blaze through her belly, and Emmett's
red leaving won't name Mamie any kind of mother.
A round-faced sugar whistler, her gone boy is
(through the stiff-clenched mouth of remembering) a
grayed and shadows child. *Listen.* She used to be pretty.
Windy days blasted her skin sweet. She was slight, brown-faced,
in every wide way the opposite of the raw, screeching thing
chaos made use of. Now, folded so small, she tires of the
sorries, the *Lawd have mercy*s. Grief's damnable tint
is everywhere, darkening days she is no longer aware of.

She is wrong-worshipped, repeatedly emptied of light, pulled
and caressed, cooed at by strangers, offered pork and taffy.
Boys stare hard at her, then snatch back their glares, as if she
killed them too, shipped them to the clutches of South. She sits,
her chair balanced on a grave's edge, and strains for sanity in
kisses upon the imagined cheek of her son. Beginning with *A*,
she recites (*angry*, *away*) the alphabet of a world gone red.
Coffee sears her throat as church ladies drift about her room,
black garb soaking their hips. They fill cups with water, drinking,
drinking in glimpses of her undoing. The absence of a black

roomful of boy is measured, again. Under the sway of coffee,
red-eyed Mamie knows their well-meaning murmur: *She*
a mama, still. You got a chile, you always a mama. Kisses
in multitudes rain from their Baptist mouths, drowning her.
Sit still, she thinks, *'til they remember how your boy was killed.*
She remembers. *Gush and implosion, crush, slippery, not boy.*
Taffeta and hymns all these women know, not a son lost and
pulled from the Tallahatchie's wretched slog. Mamie, she
of the hollowed womb, is nobody's mama anymore. She is
tinted barren. Everything about her makes the sound *sorry*.

The man-hands on her child, that dangled eye, night tumult,
things that she leans on, the only doors that open to let her in.
Faced with days and days of no him, she lets Chicago—windy,
pretty in the ways of the North—console her with boorish grays,
a stream of mourners and platters of meat to pull her through.
Is this how the backhand slap of sorrow changes the shape of a
mother? Every boy she sees now is laughing, drenched in red.
Emmett whispers *Mama, I am gold.* His bones bless the prairie.

Mammy Two-Shoes, Rightful Owner of Tom, Addresses the Lady of the House

> Mammy Two-Shoes, a character in MGM's "Tom and Jerry" cartoons, was a corpulent, achingly stereotypical black woman seen only from the knees down.

I am double negative charm, carrying the syrupy burden
of your love in my yawning breaches of body. When I laugh,
the sound is a knotted oil on each breath I draw, my lips
spread wide so you can see that my canines are obediently
filed flat—without an evident engine, my bite is no threat
to you or the lily-spiced skin of your throat. I stammer, spurt
submission and rewind, suppressing venom beneath what I'm
sure you have forgotten is an African tongue. I am master

of the google eye, manage vex and fluster when confronted
with your chirping wisdoms. I throw up my buttered
hands in surprise and joy whenever you choose to say my
given name. For the godsend of shelter and food you barely
remember not to throw away, you expect me to be a sexless
stovetop stinking of cinnamon and fat. You don't tell anyone
how inconveniently black I can be, how you have to bolt my
ghost to the kitchen floor so you can find me in the morning.

I'm only simpleminded

on cue. I have hidden in the dry dark of the pantry, weeping,
twisting the light from my fist to keep from striking you. I have
plunged chunks of bread into leaping grease and crammed
my mouth away from exploding. You believe that *yes* is the all
of my language, that I am conjured entirely of bulbous glare
and the head sag, forever on the verge of a grand gospel weep.
You want to believe that I believe that a merciful God laid me
at your feet. But there are days I feel my heart from my knees

to the tile, thudding through calves as thick as the trunks of trees,
calves kissed by the scalloped hem of a daisied apron. My chapped
heels overflow my shoes so I walk as if I was being dragged—
so, so much easier on the sole. And how many times should I
bless you for blessing me, missus, with that tomcat, scheming,
skanked and feral, flea-munched, out of his mind with motivation
and mange, how many ways can I thank you for pushing
a cat into the space where any other woman's child would be?

You gave me that look-down, a feisty relationship with the floor,
permission to wag my flabby finger at something, a little push-pull
oh no you didn't kingdom to rule, an official reason to flap my
gums and call and call on Jesus. I say *Tom, you'se in dat icebox...*
you best start to prayin'! I screech *Lawd, lawd, Thomas, is dat*
a mouse? And just like that, I'm up on a quivery dinette chair,
a chair bound to collapse with my overload, everything about
me a'jiggle, my eyes stunned like they been slapped from behind.

In twenty years, you've given me pussy and vermin, the same way
you gave me your squirming, babbling cornsilk-crowned boys, who
started their lives by scarring my breast with their blunt new teeth,
who climbed my body and rode every weary surface that
would hold them. Their stubby fingers gloppy with jelly and snot,
they pried beneath my headrag for the mystery of my hair,
scraped my forearm and cheek raw and looked for black
to be that something alive beneath their nails, and yes, they've slowly

gone stupid with the sugar, lard and mouse droppings I shovel into
their bowls, then into their mouths. And I smile. I slip a tiny razor
into the space between my teeth and the wall of my cheek, and I
smile. At night, after I loudly thank God for the each of you, I never
sleep. I shamble along the floorboards, the nosy cat licking my heels,
that mouse skittering blue beneath the stove. Sleep threatens, but I'm

careful not to swallow. Just outside your door, I listen to the capture and unlatch of your breath. I move the blade to my resting tongue.

Again, I moan *Yes* and

God says

Don't

Incendiary Art: Ferguson, 2014

they should have
left him there
to be the center
of his own altar,
shat upon, he would have flowered,
his empty hands tucked, ass upended
like a newborn
the lengthy streak of browning
blood could be a sanctified walkway
for the church ladies
for the pokers with their sticks
for the lawbreakers and abiders
for that new kinda worship

they should have
taken advantage of those
fourteen thousand
four hundred seconds and thought
it over for fourteen thousand
more
how sobering it would be
breathless icon as traffic circle
every day
Chevys and livery cabs inching
around the stain
of him   shriekers on the school bus
tasting his blossoming funk
in their clothes
having long ago given up
counting
flies

they should have
left his body
steaming on the asphalt
while passenger-side doors
wrenched from '80s sedans,
flaming barrels of garbage,
charred shards of drugstore,
and bare-chested boys, beautiful
and bulls-eyed,
blurred past in tribute

black lives
matter
most when they are in
motion, the hurtle and reverb
matter   the rushed melody of fist
the shudderings of a scorched
throat matter
the engine that moves us
toward
each damnable dawn
matters

they should have
left him there as
proof

eventually the embers would
have died
in his hair

XXXL

We've lost them all beneath those swaddling clothes.
Cavernous sweats and denims droop with air
and hide our loves inside. They strike the pose,

they cue the swagger, everybody knows
they think they're men. And yet they're wrapped with care.
We've lost them all beneath those swaddling clothes.

Inside, their bodies shudder, come to blows
with time. Their fractured lives can't reach them there.
Love hides inside. They coil, they strike. The pose,

if it is done just right, wards off the blows
that real men can see coming. Say a prayer.
We've lost them all beneath their swaddling clothes.

They've chosen this dull way to drown. That shows
it really doesn't matter that we care,
they must hide love inside. They strike the pose

of men because, as we have come to know,
no babies strut these streets—they wouldn't dare.
We've lost them all beneath their swaddling clothes.
They hide our love inside, then strike the pose.

Emmett Till: Choose Your Own Adventure

Turn to page 209 if Emmett Till's body is never found.

Our chubby grinner, just another child
who ambled into mist, no tip or trace,
no signs that he was hunted or reviled
before he turned into a jagged space
that wasn't there, then was. Nobody saw
that city boy whose swagger marked him first
as clueless, then as fool. Into the maw
of Mississippi at its very worst,
he disappeared without a single sound—
no screech or mannish giggle, wounded cry
or whistle. Mama Mamie, counting down
to zero, grasped the hands of passersby—
the white ones muttered *Girl, leave us alone.*
The Negroes said *You should have left him home.*

In February 2010, 21-year-old student Shamsiddin Abdur-Raheem abducted his 3-month-old daughter Zara. He placed her in a knapsack, drove to a bridge on the Garden State Parkway in New Jersey and threw her out of the passenger-side window of his car. She drowned in the Raritan River, more than 100 feet below.

In November 2011, also in New Jersey, Arthur Morgan III picked up his 2-year-old daughter, Tierra, for a trip to the movies. Later, Tierra was found face down in a frigid stream beneath a park overpass, strapped into a car seat that had been weighed down with a car jack. It was unclear whether she was thrown from the overpass or carried into the park and placed in the water.

The Five Stages of Drowning

Surprise

There is no drunk like the drunk of milk sleep.
A drizzled white floods the body and weighs down
everywhere we think we know about awake.
Zara's new clockwork staggers with it while Daddy,
grizzle and wild-eye, lobs her like trash over
the rusting rail. Inside the sack, the wriggling child
cannot translate *fly, plummet, descend*. She doesn't
realize the hard questions she poses for pigeons
or how, so dull and stupid with dairy, she is all
the fall the sky can language. Babies accept what

they are given. They never question the morning's
flood of sun, a kitchen's blaring stink, or the wide
hovering faces of fathers. After a swollen breeze
pries her eyes open in the few seconds it takes for

the fevered discarding of daughter, baby doesn't
ask the sun, needling light into the sack, to offer
rule or direction. Zara Malani-Lin Abdur-Raheem,
little not-bird, has been jettisoned, ditched, unloaded.
Her snared arms can find no rhyme for *wing*.
The river's glittering trash smacks her blunt,

but not before her tiny O fails its role as mouth,
not before language breaks its promise to wait
for her. If Zara can conjure no word for *word*, can
find no way to bellow *Up, Daddy, up* as she tumbles,
stuffed inside a *downdowndown* reeking so oddly
of him, how would she voice panic born of the day's
quick fist? Slapped awake, she breathes in the close
cloth and feels the little ruckus of a new heart.
The startled river opens, then closes over her, the way
a new mother would.

Involuntary Breath Holding

Imagine filling your whole body with everything you are
and then holding it there. Imagine the smallness of that body.

You are nothing but the easy of blue, red and green, food
you have smashed with your fingers, and the stumbling

possibilities of walk. Imagine not knowing that the ability
to contain all of you in tiny ballooned cheeks decides whether

you continue. Imagine not knowing the word *continue*.
Quick wisps of fish nip warily at those fat cheeks, fall into

irreparable love and decide to make a new religion of you.
Hallelujah, you are now a religion, a church of slither and slide

while Daddy roars his glee into noontime traffic, not thinking
about you, but thinking about your mother, and screeching *Oh, she*

got another man now, huh? Well, fuck that ho, I got sumthin
for her ass! Bet this gon' fix her bitch ass now, and you, Tierra,

are the fix for her ass now, you are the fix for Mama's ass now,
you are the pawn in a payback that *cannot* be unplayed. And

your daddy, now miles away from your slow plunging, does a lousy
parking job and stumbles into a smoky, red-walled gin mill

populated by other men without daughters. Hoisting a fat gold
shot, he toasts his one accomplishment—the uncomplicated

removal of a complication—while your cheeks deflate and the door
to your next minute closes. You were alive when the stream first

lapped its way 'round you, and the *d* sound comes so sweet to
the mouth of a baby who wants it. You laughed *D-Daddy* until

the giddy fish reexamined their worship of you, you coughed
Daddy Daddy until *Daddy Daddy* was nothing but sound,

then you spat *d d d* into the mud until you couldn't. The fickle
fish, back in love, kissed the place where your breath had been.

Hypoxic Convulsions

Daddy is the architect of a baby girl's roll and rock.
He teaches her to manage slink, schools her in a woman's
wet engine. If Zara lives—which she most definitely
will not—
somebody else's daddy will teach her all the one way
there is not to get lured into a sack, how to lay quietly

in the wrong skirt while her muscles argue,
how one well-timed convulsion
usually clears the dance floor. Like good drowning,
good dancing hits the backside like an annoyance
that must be watusied loose. But how to respond
to a sudden wet that's out to rearrange? Of course—
drums are injected—
and Tierra, all thrash and snapdragon,
shimmies for her giggle back. Baby is the battery
black women build their bodies around
until they're old enough to be officially romanced
by yet another revision of Jesus. But right now

they're too little to feel the full hand
of the Jesus voice, the caress of proverb and psalm.
They're flirting with that Big Daddy for all their
little worth—look at that itty jerk and boogaloo,
that pop swirling of hips they can't find, that runaway
rimshot in unfinished chests. They're rearing back,
opening wide,
rearing back, opening
wide, rearing
back, both throats
opening and slamming
shut with river.

Cue the skanky music. Brackish water snags
the rhythm, controls their arms and ankles,
gleefully involves their necks, it says

Baby,
save the last dance
for me.

Unconsciousness

The river, tho. Sluggish and cagey and habitually a bitch,
she has not decided to accept Zara, this vexation in her mouth.
She is dazzled by choke, flopped blossoms and the occasional
seduced diver, but repulsed by all frailties of skin. The river
is seldom in a mood to have her swerve scrutinized or interrupted.
Now what is this damned hindrance, keeling over in the current?
Prying the sack wide with gush, she prods the puckered contents,
is *not* entertained. Intending to add the ugly pudge to her baubles,
she finds that she cannot rouse it, is *so* not entertained. The little
blue not-fish thing is flaccid, so unfun, snazzed up in its sopping
petal pink, the eyes slit and rolling, nappy crown trapping living
things that desperately need to breathe. The hide skids and burps.
The river's most devoted feeders, so jazzed at first, have already
had a go at it. And the thing won't give the river its props, won't
beg for refuge in the water's arms, it won't *say* anything. The river
flicks a bored blue finger at it, then flicks it away. She is so *over*
this drama. Hell, the end of anything is only a kick to watch once.

Clinical Death

> The final stage in the drowning process is death. Clinical death
> occurs when both breathing and circulation stop. The victim
> is in cardiac arrest. The heart stops pumping blood. The vital
> organs are no longer receiving oxygen-rich blood. The lack of
> oxygen causes the skin to turn blue.

There are 52 shades of blue—or a million and 52, depending upon which
river you ask.

3: Cornflower.

17: Cerulean.

21: Blunt force.

28: Turquoise.

34: Navy.

37: *Fix for her bitch ass now.*

41: Sky.

47: *Goodbye*—but the way the river says it: *"Bye"*—all dismissal and shade.

52: *Goodbye*—but the way a daddy says it—over his shoulder, thrilling
the done of the deed, already mad
at the traffic.

When Black Men Drown Their Daughters

When black, men drown. They spend their whole lifetimes
justifying the gall of springing the trap, the inconvenience
of slouched denim, of coupling beyond romance or aim.
All the while, the rising murk edges toward their chins.
Hurriedly, someone crafts another scientific tome, a giddy
exploration of the curious dysfunction identifying black
men first as possible, then as necessary. Elegant equations
succumb to a river that blurs quotient and theory, rendering
them unreadable, and the overwhelm easily disappears
the men, their wiry heads glistening, then gulped. All that's
left is the fathers' last wisdom, soaked wreckage on silver:
Girl, that water ain't nothing but wet. I'm gon' be alright.

When black men drown, their daughters turn to their mothers
and ask *What should I do with this misnamed shiver in my
left shoulder? How should I dress in public?* They are weary
of standing at the shore, hands shading their eyes, trying
to make out their own fathers among the thousands bobbing
in the current. The mothers mumble and point to any flailing
that seems familiar. Mostly, they're wrong. Buoyed by church
moans and comfort food of meat and cream, the daughters
try on other names that sound oddly broken when pressed
against the dank syllables of the fathers'. Drained, with just
forward in mind, they walk using the hip of only one parent.
They scratch in their sleep. Black water wells up in the wound.

When black men drown, their daughters are fascinated with
the politics of water, how gorgeously a surface breaks
to receive, how it weeps so sanely shut. And the thrashing
of hands, shrieking of names: *I was Otis, I was Willie Earl,
they called me Catfish.* Obsessed by the waltzing of tides,

the daughters remember their fathers—the scorch of beard
electrifying the once-in-a-while kiss, the welts in thick arms,
eyes wearied with so many of the same days wedged behind
them. When black men drown, their daughters memorize all
the steps involved in the deluge. They know how long it takes
for a weakened man to dissolve. A muted light, in the shape
of a little girl, used to be enough to light a daddy's way home.

When black men drown, their daughters drag the water's floor
with rotting nets, pull in whatever still breathes. They insist their
still-dripping daddies sit down for cups of insanely sweetened
tea, sniffs of rotgut, tangled dinners based on improbable swine.
The girls hope to reacquaint their drowned fathers with the concept
of body, but outlines slosh in drift and retreat. The men can't get
dry. Parched, they scrub flooded hollows and weep for water
to give them name and measure as mere blood once did. Knocking
over those spindly-legged dinette chairs, they interrupt the failed
feast and mutter *Baby girl, gotta go, baby gotta go*, their eyes
misted with their own murders. Grabbing their girls, they spit
out love in reverse and stumble toward the banks of some river.

When black men drown their daughters, the rash act is the only
plausible response to the brain's tenacious mouth and its dare: *Yes,
yes, open your ashed hands and release that wingless child.* Note
the arc of the sun-drenched nosedive, the first syllable of the child's
name unwilling from the man's mouth, the melody of billow that
begins as blessed clutch. Someone crouching inside the father waits
impatiently for the shutting, the lethargic envelop, and wonders if
the daughter's wide and realizing eye will ever close to loose him.
It never will, and the man and his child and the daughter and her
father gaze calmly into the wrecked science of each other's lives.
The sun struggles to spit a perfect gold upon the quieting splash.
The river pulses stylish circles of its filth around the swallow.

Blurred Quotient and Theory

My mother and father fought like there was one
breath in the room and only one throat could have
it. They fought like Crisco and a scarlet skillet,
like cold hose-spray fights with cats coupling
in a night alley. All day they walked gingerly on
their raised fists, all night she played 'bama pure
until Otis Redding lit their hips and nasty flecks
of old tobacco flowed from his gold tooth to hers.
They spat backwood, each one craving all the South
in the other. One of them regretted me. And it was
that one who fixed her mouth to say *Get on outta
here, Otis*, and after that my father lived in one place

and me in another. All my friends who were girls
had a father living in one place while they lived
in another, and if you were a girl, that was alright.
Girls needed their mamas. *There my daddy go right
there* was the chime, with a fingerpoint at the corner
store, at a passenger-side rider in a passing Buick,
at a smoky figure slipping into some other door,
at a worker swinging his lunch bucket, at a hooter
in sharkskin whistling at somebody else's mama,
at a man getting his face slapped with cologne after
a haircut, at a dice game winner in Garfield Park,
and sometimes this sadness: *Well, I* think *that's him.*

Sometimes a daughter is simply what the middle
of a crib does. Later, she becomes the opener
of doors. She warms that plate of neckbones,
and pirouettes for his gaze. Sometimes she is the spit

of the mother, the irritant prancing the outer edge
of rooms, the cheek roughly pinched, the handful
of dimes and *Go on, get yourself some Red Hots*,
the math problem one person in class keeps getting
wrong, the *Sit on in here and be still while your mama
and I*—Sometimes she is sometimes. She is an oddity,
or she is air. What Tierra was was shatter to anyone
doomed enough to love her. What Zara was was not a son.

Sagas of the Accidental Saint

For the mothers of the lost

I don't expect you'll recognize my voice.
I don't believe this saga I've suppressed
will ever sound familiar. I am just

a stooped and accidental saint, no choice
except to strain the limits of my throat.
I am the mama weep beneath the fold,

that paragraph you skip, the wink of gold
inside a rotted mouth, that shredding note
of grief. Excuse what's inexcusable

in me—the shifting wildfire-tinted weave,
my ankles blue with fluid, how I grieve
in gospel you can't clutch—a fusible

display of doubled negatives I spew
whenever someone says my child is gone
and then goes on to pile the blame upon

my child for being gone. Or maybe you
believe the wretched mess is rightly traced
right back to *me*, whose body housed the crime—

my daughter out of dollars, out of time,
my son just seeking ways to be erased.
So many ways they stride into the line

of gunfire, tease the trigger, crave the shot,
just living through their days as if they're not
about to die. He totes a paper bag of wine,

or tussles, laughing, with his kid or rolls
a joint or asks his boo to braid his hair
while lazing on the stoop, or dares to glare

when someone shoves. She fights against the holds
around her throat or somehow looks the same
as someone else or sits inside her car

or someone else's car, or leaves ajar
a door she should have closed. He plays a game
of hoops to clear his head, or doesn't raise

his hands, or raises them, or doesn't stop
or does, or, when commanded, fails to drop
his wallet, keys or phone. He sets ablaze

a heap of trash, somebody's car or store,
while shouting slogans meant to make you care
that he's alive. She's killed if she's not there

although she said she'd be, or there before
she should have been, or on her way to work,
or coming home not walking like she should,

not walking down the street she normally would.
He walks too close behind, you have to jerk
your purse out of the way, you palm the mace,

he passes, spitting lyric vile and blue,
not giving damns that he's offending you.
All you can remember is his race.

You ask him to succumb, he dares decline,
the situation quickly falls apart.
A weapon's raised to line up with his heart

because he feels entitled to his spine.
She fumbles in her pocket for some change
or jumps the A train turnstile on a dare.

She mumbles like her mind is not all there,
or titters in a way you think is strange.
He wrecks his Chevy, waves for help, he calls

the 9 the 1, the 1. He's *waiting* wrong,
the folks around him said he didn't belong.
He coughs or sneezes, looks away, he brawls

with brothers, sisters, father, wife. He waves
a Walmart toy, or he can't find his place
in line, he laughs too loud, he can't retrace

his steps, he droops his pants, he misbehaves.
She turns her back or whirls around or could
be packin', could be wanted, could be strong

enough to snap your neck. She moves all wrong.
He wanders into someone else's hood
in colors that he struggles to explain.

He prances, strides, he's plotting an escape,
he stops and spins on you, he's here to rape
your daughter. Or he scoffs when you complain

about his smell, he crafts a sign, he parks
behind your Chevy, thrusts his massive fist
into or through the air, he wakes up pissed

but right on time, then smokes a blunt or arcs
his brow when someone asks *You good?* He waits
his turn or takes a break, he takes a leak,

he frightens everyone with his physique,
the situation's bound to escalate.
So many ways they're asking not to be.

She's wearing out her welcome, being black
when no one's asked her to, you've seen her lack
of grace, the space she occupies, her glee

when chicken, weed or welfare checks roll in.
He goes to class, he graduates, he takes
the seat right next to you, his shoulder makes

you quake inside. You simply don't know when
he'll blow. She shops beneath the winking eye
of video, but then pays with a card

that *can't* be hers. His chest and arms are scarred
with scrape and blood tattoos—so why untie
the noose shaped like his neck? His clothes are blue

or red, he wants your job, he's scoped your wife,
he craves your home, your cash, your perfect life,
that textbook in his hand's not fooling you.

She hawks and spits, she begs for change, she blows
a harp, she blows through blow, she blows her chance,
a victim, yet again, of circumstance.

He's fighting back, but everybody knows
that he's too coarse, too dumb, too street, too black,
too dense, too doomed, too thick, too much of those,

too vicious pose, too quick to come to blows,
too likely he could spark your heart attack.
He flares his nostrils, hides his hands, he flees

without explaining why. She lifts, she steals,
she swipes, she grabs, she snatches, cuts a deal.
He stumbles, trips, he trips a wire, he sees

too much, she needs too much, he feels too much,
her skin's too mud, his skin's too light, he fights
too dirty, fights for breath, the savage nights

are huge with him, the voodoo in his touch—
he shoots himself while handcuffed to a pole,
or hangs himself while hanging from a tree,

or wrings his neck although his hands aren't free.
He always seems to fail at self-control.
He's monster, ogre, he's the looming threat,

insisting he didn't do that thing he did,
denying that she'd hidden what she hid,
confusing you by getting so upset.

He claims he's innocent, he files a case,
he lives too large, too long, he must believe
that he is white or free. He's so naive—

with every step he takes, he falls from grace.
He steps inside or out, or through or down,
she bellows, jumps or hisses, struts or spins,

he stalks a street, steps off a curb. His sins
should be enough to drive him out of town,
where he'd be out of sight and out of mind

and out of bounds but thankfully not out
of range. And if you think he's all about
the kill, the drops, the guns and gangster grind,

you know for sure as soon as you see me—
his mama, grieving ugly, wailing 'bout
my chile, my chile, and plucking Jesus out

of every bag. You just can't see why he
deserves such stupid love—my wailing thrusts,
each *Lord have mercy on my baby's soul*,

my sad theatrics as my child goes cold.
And then the hungry cameras readjust
my howls—until it's not my child who's dead,

but something feral, edged in leak, a threat
to shrubbery and Sundays. While he's wet
and seeping into street, they frame his head

and mine inside a single shot and ask
my nappy hair and bulging eyes just what
I think. I keen, implode on cue. They cut

the camera back to frame the blooded mask
and splay. You don't remember what I say,
or hear his name, but you are borderline

obsessed with my collapse, my crumpled whine
and holy-ghosted flail, the matinee
of mama. You are entertained until

you aren't. And then I'm just an open maw,
a blur and tongue. You shouldn't waste your awe
on my unleashed display of overkill.

Ignore the blackish bruiser, dripping bile,
the spittle-spewing me, still bellowing
my Lord my Lord why would you let this thing

disrupt your day? I disappear. And while
I'm relegated to an anecdote
on way to nothing, all you can recall

is sputtered gospel woe and caterwaul,
that corpse the tightened wire around my throat.

that's my son collapsed there my son
crumpled there my son lying there
my son positioned there my daughter
repositioned there my daughter as
exhibit A there my daughter dumped
over there my son hidden away there
my son blue there my son dangling
there my son caged there my daughter
on the gurney there on the slab there
in the drawer there my daughter splayed
there my son locked down there my
son hanging there my son bleeding
out there my son growing frigid there
my daughter deposited there my son
inside the chalk there my daughter
being bagged there my son on the slab
there my son crushed there my son
rearranged there my son crumpled
in the door there my daughter's neck
shrinking in the noose there my son's
left eye over there my son as exhibit B
there my son behind the wheel there
my son under the wheels there my son
slumped over the wheel there my son

my daughter blooded and not moving
in the doorway on the stoop down
the block in front of her kids just inside
the barbershop facedown in the street
outside the bodega inside the bodega
in the black alley behind the bodega
on the videotape a block from home
leaving home hanging out at home
in the schoolyard on the blacktop
in his bed in her kitchen in my arms
in my arms in my arms that's my son
shot to look thug that's my daughter
shot to look more animal shot as kill
shot as prey shot as conquest shot as
solution shot as lesson shot as warning
shot as comeback shot as payback shot
for sport shot for history that's my son
not being alive any more there that's my
child coming to rest one layer below
the surface of the

rest

of my life

there

August 19, 2014, St. Louis, MO--Kajieme Powell, 25, was
accused of shoplifting donuts and energy drinks. Police
said the mentally disturbed man approached with a knife "in
an overhand grip"—they shot him dead 15 seconds after they
arrived. Video shows that Powell's hands were at his side.

I am the mother of that darkest magician. His thousand
limbs thrash in and out of your practiced sightline.
He is always behind, beside and in front of you.
He lunges for your neck while whistling on a side street
three blocks away. Firepower throbs in every finger
of his bound or idle hands. No matter where he is,
he is the leading man in the stuttering convenience store video

If he is not there,

> he will be.

If he hasn't,

> he is about to.

If a blade's not in his hand, it's

> in his hand.

If his hands are up,
they're clawing through his pockets

> for

something.

If he's screeching *Don't shoot!*

> he's clearly saying
> *Please. I'm tired. Help me fall down.*

228

December 2, 2014, Phoenix AZ--Rumain Brisbon, 34, an
unarmed father of four, was shot to death when a police
officer mistook a bottle of pills for a gun.

The son of the mother of mistake, he was
clearly saying
Please.
I'm tired.
Help me fall down.

Nothing in that bottle could end his
hurting quicker than that one stormy
lyric turning final in his chest.
His hundred fingers were stumblers,
dark and probably. My children
are blasted daily out of their own
names, paying with breath for the sin
of pockets. And wallets. And bottles.
And phones. And toys. Choking on
the iron stench of blood, he reached
for the day after the one he was falling in.
Nothing good was there. Nothing good
ever reached back.

March 3, 2014, Iberia Parish, LA--Police say that Victor
White III, 22, shot himself while handcuffed in the back of
a police cruiser.

November 19, 2013, Durham, NC--Police say that Jesus
Huerta, 17, shot himself while handcuffed in the back of a
police cruiser.

July 29, 2012, Jonesboro, AR--Police say that Chavis
Carter, 21, shot himself while handcuffed in the back of
a police cruiser.

He reached back and found
his own hands with his own
hands, worked his bound
fingers to set his free fingers
loose, then used that shackled
hand to free the other shackled
hand, and the freed shackled
hand, still shackled, was still
bound to the other hand once
both were freed. Once free
in the shackles, the shackled
hands turned to the matter
of the gun, which couldn't be
there because they'd searched
my baby twice and a gun is
a pretty big thing unless it isn't,
unless it is dreamed alive by
hands that believe they are no
longer shackled. Stunned in
cuffs, but free and searching,
the left and right hands found
a gun with a stink like voodoo,

a gun that couldn't have been
there, wasn't there, but was.
The left-handed him used
a cuffed hand, which could
have been either left or right
(since both were free), to root
around for a trigger and fire
a bullet right into his left-
handed head, impossible but
not really, since the preferred
killing hand may have preferred
its shackles. The policemen,
who had searched my baby
twice and cuffed both his free
and unfree hands behind his
back before his hands found
his own hands and pulled,
heard no human sound at all
during all that frantic magic,
no *Fuck!* as my boy struggled
to get his left shackled hand
to do what his right shackled
hand wouldn't do, no frenzied
pound of one bracing foot
against the door, no grunt
or whoop of glee to mark all
those times he slipped out
of custody and in again. But
they did hear the bang
of the gun that wasn't there
(but was) just when it sent
that bullet into the right side
of his left-handed head. *Sounds
like sacrifice*, they thought.

Slumped, eyes cocked and
undone, my child was amazed
at the sweet hoodoo he had
managed. Both left and right
hands were shackled and free
behind him, there was an eerie
perfect circle of smoke in his
hair. *Suicide*, they both said at
the very same time, and since
it was odd how they had reached
the same conclusion, they smiled
and shook their heads. Noting
the shackles, they praised their
God in the light of miracle while
the boy who couldn't have done
what he did, but did, bled down
to zero. *Guess he couldn't take it,*
one of the alive said to the other.
He didn't mean wearing the shackles.
He meant not wearing them.

March 15, 2012, Queens, NY--Shereese Francis, 30, a
schizophrenic, had stopped taking her medications and
needed an ambulance. Police arrived, handcuffed an agitated
Shereese, and held her face down on a mattress until she
went into cardiac arrest and stopped breathing.

She couldn't get out from under the venom
flooding the muscle across the span of her back,
the command that she *Breathe!* from a growler
with both knees on her breath. She couldn't
summon the spit she needed to call out for me
or debate the hammers taking flower behind
her eyes. With flecks of his spit in her perm
and a prickly pressure suppressing her spine,
maybe she thought that the abrupt theft of beat
was how Jesus ended mayhem in the body—
with all the mayhem at once and then none.
Her life, relived at its end, unreeled as brash
cinema. It was lucid, as bright as backhand:

A pair of patent leather Mary Janes with taps
and gilded buckles. A walk through a hundred
songs with half her heart, all the swerve, all
sugar intact. A laugh with an open mouth. Even
when her mind careened and fled for tumbling
lights, she was my child. She hurtled forward
from my body, and her living was a struggle
to clutch. I loved her beauty. I loved her unkilled.

June 22, 2007, West Memphis, AR--DeAunta Terrell Farrow,
12, was gunned down by police officer Erik Sammis, who
claimed that only after he shot Farrow did he realize that
the gun the child was carrying was a toy.

Even mamas were 12 once, screeching
glee and unkilled. I skipped in All Stars.
Even girls who became mamas once had
silver toy pistols that spat sparks to startle

the church ladies. We hung plastic handcuffs
from our belts and hurled rock-hard balls
at each other's bellies and heads. There
were knots, sometimes blood, on our lips.

We made our mouths make sounds like
bullets, we dodged fun that was out to break
us. Drunk on that little glee, we murdered
and murdered and murdered each other.

Like Tom, that cartoon cat, we collapsed,
unblooded, our skulls turned completely
around, bulged eyes on the ground by our
heads, our ears blown off. But we got up,

ready to be killed again. Again. We had all
seen Tom shotgunned, knifed, beheaded,
bitten, poisoned, exploded. Once, he was
misled by a cooing puss in a snug skirt,

and his heart broke out right through his
chest. A little surprised every time he died,
but unfazed by his resurrections, he'd brush
it off, reattach his head, lick his paw, smooth

his fur like *That's all you got?* So, like him,
I made a game out of losing and finding my
life. I fell and fell and got back up, corduroys

stiff, knees throbbing with scrape. I sprang
right up, swinging swears, already running
through a lengthy laundry list of vengeance,
every sweet payback ending with *You dead!*

Lay down! Yes, I fell down dead, but I
always popped right back up, maybe a little
closer to dying, but still 12, as certain as
black cats, and, in the end, utterly alive.

That's why I arched over his body, willing
his leaks to seal, praying him into a wacky
and improbable cartoon resurrection,
into *Get up, get up, get up, please get*
up, but then the credits rolled, which meant
the day was fresh out of his brand of breath—

even his color

began to leave.

November 19, 2011, White Plains, NY--The LifeAid medical
alert bracelet of Kenneth Chamberlain Sr., 68, was
triggered by mistake. When the police responded, he
refused to open the door to his apartment, saying he did
not need help. A LifeAid recording captured Officer Steven
Hart calling him a "nigger." After working for an hour to
force open the door, the police broke it down, tasered
Chamberlain and shot him dead.

My son was hunched vintage, a nighttime.
You need our help, boy, you need our help.
He placed a finger on his slow-throbbing
neck, knew for a fact that his heart still
knew its right place beneath his shirt.
*You just don't know you need our help, let
us in, let us in.* He couldn't say no enough,
hating the old Negro waver in the word.
*Let us into your gas stove, your couch, your
nasty tousled bed, your rat skittering blue
note behind the trash.* That damned rat, all
the music he had. *Your heart's not right,
you're running a fever, nigger.* Where was he,
Mississippi? Was he a boy, barefoot again,
running wild for no reason, pounding
all that red dust dizzy? Was he on fire
again? *You feel hot through this wood.*

     We're here to help
his heart clenched
     we're here to fall you down
and the fire walked a road
     to fall you down
through my child's body
     to stop your worry

and straight up to
  nigger, to fix your life
that moon
  to make it right
he always watched
  to give you rest
and wanted

March 24, 2012, Pasadena, CA--Kendrec McDade, 19, was
chased and shot seven times by two police officers after a
911 caller falsely reported being robbed at gunpoint by two
black men. McDade's final words were "Why did they shoot me?"

As the moon tangled its beams and grew
monstrous huge over his body, he wanted
that answer. As usual, I arrived too late—
he had already dispersed, and become an
awkward hour. Son of the mother of mistake,
his timing and root were askew. But

*because walk because upright because Africa because decision because Tuesday
because loaded gun because running because two black because identified because
uniform because breathless because unable because America because yo mama
because Mississippi because uniform because Obama because the chase because
unarmed because convenient because mistaken because threatened because ritual
because no one will miss you because beast because innocent because they could
because they could because they could because they could because they—*

I usually give my boys names anybody can remember.
Scapegoat. Target. PerpWalk. HeDidIt. Oversight.
The name Kendrec so quashed his potential. He should
have been *Victim. Identify. Bullseye. NotAgain.*
Miracle. 2BlackMenWithAGun. How about—

Accident.
Perfect.

I never had children.

I just had accidents.

```
September 14, 2013, Bradfield Farms, NC--After being
involved in a traffic accident, Jonathan Ferrell, 24,
knocked on the door of a nearby house for help. The woman
inside called the police. They arrived and shot him ten
times.
```

My son said: *I just had an accident. I need to use a phone.*
She said: *You're black.*
My son said: *It'll only take a minute. I need to call the police.*
She heard: *Call the police.*
My son said: *I know it's late, but—I just had an accident.*
She said: *911.*
He said: *OK, then. You'll call 911?*
She said: *You're black.*
The police said: *Is he black?*
She said: *He's black.*
When the gun arrived, it said *I just had an accident.*

The gun said: *I just had an accident.*

The gun said: *I just had an accident.*

The gun said: *I just had an accident.*

The gun said: *I just had an accident.*

The gun said: *I just had an accident.*

The gun said: *I just had an accident.*

The gun said: *I just had an accident.*

The gun said: *I just had an accident.*

The gun said: *I just had an accident.*

March 21, 2012, Chicago, IL--Rekia Boyd, 22, was killed
by off-duty police detective Dante Servin. Saying he saw
someone pull a gun and point it at him, Servin fired five
rounds over his left shoulder, through his car window, into
a crowd. Boyd was struck in the back of the head. The gun
Servin saw was actually a cell phone.

He just had an accident. Every shuffled air
is stumbling and probably. And there was
Rekia, knotted in a black flow that conjured
the idea of army. He smelled them at his back
and knew he would never have survived their
intent with only the thin wall of a car around him.

If they haven't,

                 they are about to.   The glint.

If a gun's not in his hand,

                 it's in his hand.   The slow

menace of how they meant his end.

If a bullet's not in the barrel   The fierce

                 it's in the air   whipping

to nape of neck
to her slow unloosing box braid
to jaw muscle
to the snap of
his New Era fitted,

to Indian Remy
to the spine's sweet tip
to a turned back

                              you know
sometimes they don't find
the whole head

once it is mist,
it drips from chainlink
seeps into asphalt
clogs storm drains

becomes
too fluid
for me

          to mourn

February 28, 2003, Las Vegas, NV--Orlando Barlow, 28, was
surrendering on his knees in front of four police officers
when one of them shot him with an assault rifle from 50 feet
away. Barlow was unarmed. The officer said he was afraid
that Barlow was faking surrender. Federal investigators
later discovered that the same officers had printed T-shirts
labeled "bdrt," for "Baby Daddy Removal Team."

He obediently folded to his knees, slow-stuttering
Yes sir yes sir yes sir yes sir like I taught him,
sinking deep, kingmaker, his eyes locked on all
of them and every single one of them at the same
time. Stifling muscle, he made himself small,
suppressed the red of crushing their Adam's apples
with the chapped heel of his hand. He could have
stood wide up and become their worst wall. Instead
he succumbed. He was safe until they began circling,
slow like blaze's first lap at wood, and one of them
zoned in on that sweet spot, that deep blue dip
in his chest that so loud and plainly uttered
Animal.

I also became the mother of the sons and daughters
of my daughters and sons. I am their silvering
nana, plucking sweaty wads of ones from my
bra to pay for rattles and Enfamil and bags
of fluorescent cheese curls because getting drunk
on the orange dust is the only thing that will
calm them. I am the grandmother who becomes
the mother of the flails, squeals and belching
my darling corpses leave behind, *I get up, get
up*, without words replacing what has been
removed. I am a saint quite accidentally, a tired
woman piecing together soldiers who were once

pieced together by the soldiers who were born
to me. My arms are thinned by their pull. I can
only hold on until they find the door I've so
willfully locked, and they burst through. And Lord,
they're armed with what they think are the rules.

July 18, 2011, Denver, CO--Alonzo Ashley, 29, who may
have been suffering from mental illness, refused to stop
splashing his face at a Denver Zoo drinking fountain on a
blistering hot day, then made irrational comments and threw
a trash can. Admitting that he was unarmed, officers killed
him with a Taser, citing his "extraordinary strength."

Lord, what are the rules? On the devil's day,
can't a black man stop and scrub off some
season? Can't he talk his core down without
officially explaining? It's not like anyone but
his mama would understand the flow of sweat
beneath his sweat, the outright music his head
told him it's time to and damned alright to sing.

But his corded forearms, the muscle pushing
forward the fix in his eyes, the flared snort
and snot and brick of him. The clenched ass,
the impatient neck, the resplendent neck,
the sweat-crusted neck, the gorgeous neck,
the mad you made him as the heat blew hard
on his tangle, his terrible vast, his towering.
His breath blasting flat and meat like my pot
liquor, his thighs telling the stories of trees.
His thread spiraling too fast aloose. Is what
you saw. Is what you saw. Even though my
boy was light enough to be lifted by a notion,
you punched him with holes so everything
that said *man* aloud would gush out. Murder

helps you sleep at night. Murder
keeps me up at night, thinking of you
asleep at night.

February 8, 2015, Fairfax County, VA--Suffering from mental illness, Natasha McKenna died after being shocked four times with a stun gun while her hands were cuffed and her legs shackled.

I am the mother of the dark magicians,
but sometimes the magic loses its holy
clutch. Natasha should have been able
to slip those shackles long enough to
fire a bullet into the wrong side of her
hair, which would have simplified
the paperwork and left me with a body
unburned to bless. How could she forget
the hoodoo that she knew so well,
breaking loose to be the agent of her
own recapture, hanging herself with
hands that are both free and shackled?
It pains me to think of how she drowned
so utterly in spitted light. If only she
weren't so my accident, I could have
been the hands at her sides. But they
had already chalked her up to fireworks,
and my prayer, the flinging of expletives
into her waning smoke, had nowhere
to go. She wouldn't have recognized my voice.

Once I put this baby in the ground, I'm ready. . . . This means war.
—Geneva Reed-Veal, mother of Sandra Bland, addressing the
     congregation at Johnson-Phillip All Faiths Chapel, Prairie View,
     Texas

I don't expect you'll recognize my voice,
no matter that I populate your world
with demons and obstructions, dangerous
assumptions. I'm the mother of the hung,
the misted head, the pistol-whipped, the hands
that found the hands, the tasered crazy girl
and all the magic real that you can stand.
I thought perhaps I'd let you see that I
am flesh and bone and pulse, that in the night
I wail with want of them. And yes, I know
I entertain you, digitized, my break
and fall rewound, replayed and tabbed. But
now, I fight my own collapse, that ugly twist
that grief brings to my face to make you laugh.
I'm here to say their bodies weren't at war
with you. I'm here to say their bodies weren't
at war with you. I'm here to say their wars
were in their bodies. And the battlefield
was always yours, was always yours, was all.

The First 23 Minutes of the First Day Without

1. The weather is writ large through the appearance of symptoms:
2. an orange chill, the taxi driver grimacing
3. when he hears your nasty address, muttering
4. *That place is bad* Your mother absent-
5. mindedly rubbing your leg, wondering when
6. you'll get snotty and wobble-eyed   whether you'll
7. hog the limelight by flaunting your ugly blossom
8. of grief   a sin for the daughter to wear the wool
9. of widow
10. Her mantra, *He in heaven now He in heaven now*, synced
11. perfectly to the ruts in the street   The cab blares
12. black cardamom and onion, and the driver's
13. eyes widen as he enters the riotous fringe of
14. *the bad place*   barred
15. Baptist lean-tos   glint
16. snarlers arching toward the windshield   stores
17. selling wax lips and 45s   he
18. stops
19. and there is a sidewalk that still bears the slight
20. weight of your father   there is a row
21. of open mouths   *nonono*   there is a trumpeting sun
22. one whole damn day
23. behind the news

And He Stays Dead

You can convince your young body to slide on the cloak of savage—
bare your teeth towards the clock and pretend you don't feel the hollow.

Or you can slap your own face, winding back time, beating yourself
witless until years blur and you convince yourself it isn't real. The hollow

is not menaced by your trilling. It decides to take your body inside it.
You pile on layers of woolens and fiction, trying to appeal to the hollow

as it owns you. Everyone asks *Why is your voice so drained, so moon?*
It's because you are feverishly slipping on mantras that should heal the hollow,

but it just grows larger, and you flail around inside it. It is shaped so
stupidly like a father. You can't find your knees to kneel. The hollow

will be damned if it gives you a chance to pray your way out, so you
will yourself limp and succumb to damage. Passing days seal the hollow.

Daughter, wear your father like a cloak. Flaunt the blue, the gone
stink of him. Those woes are yours, crafted to reveal. You're hollow.

Emmett Till: Choose Your Own Adventure

Turn to page 258 if Emmett Till never set foot in the damned store.

So our Chicago kid runs past the store
instead of being wooed by chewing gum
and peppermints. The steamy shop's a bore
'cause they've got better suckers where he's from.
He's sworn to be remembered in this town,
and so his raucous cousins egg him on
to escapades much sweeter than those found
in candy—live and buzzing skins upon
the water, fruit to yank from every tree.
He hurtles past without a second thought,
without acknowledging her silent plea
behind the screen, her gaze so clearly fraught
with crave. *Hey nigger, welcome to the South—*
come slip my sugar deep into your mouth.

Incendiary Art: The Body

I've nightmared your writhe, glum
fists punching their way out of your
own body, the blind stumble through
the buckled vein of your throat as
your nerve endings sputtered and blew.
I've dipped my finger into a vaporous
pool of your skin. The heat blessed
your whole new self with horizon,
square-jawed boy. With such potent
intent, you blared illicit and just enough
saint. Now, with so many northern
days between us, you are much easier
to God. But they are looking for you.
They are wildly sloshing fuel across
the landscape and they are screeching
your name. Today, one said *I sure would
like to burn a black man alive.* So, yep,
you left us here with undulating acres
of fools and that particular stank leg
of gospel. You left us all this snuff,
hawk and proud little bowleg, you left
their brains stunned by dairy and fat
meat. You left us not much path, even
after your body was that brief beauteous
torch. They seem to remember you
fondly. And there are unstruck matches
everywhere.

Unshuttered, 2023

The poet wonders if the pictures are a way of making up for all the "poor down South" relatives that went un-introduced because of her mother's shame. There are hundreds and hundreds of the images now, lost-ago kinfolk flashing judgment, dimming with distance, loving on her without reason or reserve. The poet glues together a family, a warm chorus of ancestors, and her backdrop becomes a wall. How piteous, how remarkable, how magic. In them she sees the nose her mother wanted to destroy, she sees her own brown sparkless eyes, she sees the same stubborn hair hard-scorched to proper. *But those are strangers! You don't know those people, you can't know their voices!* And somewhere behind a heavy door, a concerned group of white men know that if they can just disappear that kind of desperate remembering, we will die.

1

You crush me with your damning glimpses, Anna. You,
so rancorous, so wounding, and so cruelly bred
to stain a man with scarring he won't see. Unsaid,
my reckless want of you—this yearning, thirsting, blue
inside these hands—is seed for malady, the mud
that clogs my throat, a pantomime of moan and knees.
Go home, you growl. I slip by agonized degrees
into the sound. You mouth my name, unlatching flood.

I beg you, Anna, search for mercy—heave my hurt
and humbled body close, let pity drive your slight
unwilling hips into the waiting, sweated blight
of mine. Let loose that rasping whisper—*Shed your shirt*—
and raze me slow, your mouth demolishing the rest
of who I am, until I gasp defeat against
the firelight in your neck. I just can't see the sense
in your bedevilment. What keeps you so possessed

by whiter gazes, dreaming you're the fool of those
who'd ravish without wonder? Come home to the skin
you know. Come staunch this mayhem with the medicine
inside your sacred hold, give me what you suppose
that white man craves. Oh Anna, drop me to my knees
and call the shaming love. By now, I must have riled
you past vexation into wanting. If not, I'll
crouch here in blue, content to be your wreckage.

Please.

4

I

She's buttoned   and laced up   so   stiff

staged   so black and   (whew, Lord she)   *mad*   the photographer   asks   (asks!)
me   to sit   *please ma'am*   gleams   at my bound

chest   and my sister   I swear she   sucks all that mad through her teeth
like a sow

ugly
    and   *mad*

he stands her   over me   like   a man would stand
pushes her limbs   where he
wants them   laughs   when light won't
crawl   through her hair

                                    look at that chile
looking just like
   whosoever her damn black daddy
was
guess ain't no harm
      in loving her plain ass
          even tho

II

I always know the very second she decides to believe
she can love me. She shudder-sighs, and her tight little
lips twitch, like Mary when she first saw that cross

and knew what it meant. Oh, how my sister has sacrificed
to weep woe under the millstone of me, poking at my face
for a disappeared link to our mother, for any reason

at all to declare me mistake instead of sister. She hates
knowing that I'm alive because our mother dropped and found
what she desired in the dirt, when a long-ago weather rose up

and took hold of her thighs and hands. My sister's white
daddy was a thief who ran away with what he left behind.
She and I stare at the camera. Every gone father glares back.

Evans   Sun   Finish   MIDDLETOWN, N. Y.

8

cane, cravats, and corsets tell   and retell   the body's story   the shell   we
shroud in   guile, romance, and thread   i was a doll   i was a sleek fool   i
was publicly foppish   loud as a lit lamp   but   my shoes, their upturned toes

dust and scruff   *a negro's always got nigger somewhere on 'im   all you gots to
do is*

Look

They couldn't let me occur   not like   this   not
this me   not my Sunday self   not   not like upright   not like stroll   like
matchstick   Like *la-di-fuckin'-da   boy   gotta find a crime   for you*
their rhythm partial to the red air   down around my knees
she/point//shriek//point//shriek/she/ the point is   i was where i was
         when i was there
it's true my eyes   may have swept   a woman   an hour   idea   or   a

future
                  i didn't own   she/point/she   who knew   that
there that boy is that the boy yessir that the boy   could be a whole   trial
sometimes even christians   get necks wrong   i was not *that boy*

i   used to twirl a   walking stick   and dip   my crown toward a sun   that
relished
my body

but
when we forget   that fancy only rolls
         one way

      some   body
                  reminds

                  us

267

13

We ache for fiction etched in black and white. Our eyes
never touch. These tragic grays and bustles, mourners'

hats plopped high upon our tamed but tangled crowns, strain
to disguise what yearning does with us. The white man

sputters, angered by our stiff distance: *Drape your right
arm there, across her shoulder! Move! Move in closer!*

*You're cousins, sisters, servants in the same house? Why
stand so far apart? Like strangers? Here!* Paralyzed,

mute, I try to crush the memories of your mouth's
sly moonlit trip down a trail to the center of

this body—just another complication I
will have to die to forget. And I cannot move

my hand, so terrified am I of unleashing
the howl it must conceal when your swept glance—*That's it,*

now look at her!—thunders in my neck. I want this
done. I want to own this flat fixed sentence of tin

so that everyone can take as gospel this chilled
restraint, and we can just keep on whisper-living

our lush life—which we will, whenever the night, our
blacker sister, indulges us and cloaks the moon.

Our past has done such awkward work. The rules make food of wounding.

In a large bowl, sift together the flour, baking powder, salt, and sugar.

Puppeteer, he bangs my head to tilt it. I look like a dog who hears a sound.

Make a well in the center and pour in the milk, eggs, and melted butter.

This stool staggers.
When it collapses, I will flail and nigger-beam whole perfect kitchens.

Mix until smooth.

His fingers minstrel my shoulders. Beneath this frothy skirt, hair needles
the gingham. A cock is shamed and sweating.

Heat a lightly oiled griddle or frying pan over medium-high heat.

A cock is shamed and sweating.

*Pour or scoop the batter onto the griddle, using approximately 1/4 cup
for each pancake.*

Anything for guzzle. Anything with an improbable side of swine.
Anything at all for the American mouth.

Brown on both sides

They argued. Was there enough kneel in my face?

and serve hot.

He smacks me again, adjusts the volume on my shit-eating grin.

His hand begins to mean that he is hungry.

You can move, he says, *when the box of us is perfect.*

16

Conjuring a woman is maddening. Such feeble guarantees.
I dare first what is needed—the store-bought blouse, its
treasured frill and stiff curl of cotton. The bogus bar of gold
greening at my throat. I dare sugar in practiced poses while
three overlooked hairs waggle on my chin and light struggles
through these flawed hillsides of hair—hair oiled heavy
and parted toward a quite uncertain she. What a weak
and reckless way to step forward—sitting on my hands
to quiet their roped veins and ungirled work, hiding blunt
mannish nails, bitten just this morning to a troubled blood.
I hiss-suck every air while the button on my skirt strains
and my thick toes, accustomed to field, spread slow purple
and bawl in these beautiful borrowed shoes. I sit taller,
name myself crepe myrtle, camellia, burst of all hue.

Tell me that I have earned at least this much woman. Tell me
that this day is worth all the nights I wished the muscle
of myself away. It will take mother less than a second to know
her only child, her boisterous boy, steady pounding at his
shadow to make it new. Here I am, Mama, vexing your savior,
barely alive beneath face powder and wild prayer. Here I am,
both your daughter and your son, stinking of violet water.

Walter Noel, Wytheville,
VIRGINIA.

If you want to know how much escaping never ends,
I just might be able to help you understand it.
Early one March, a drizzly Monday morning it was,
almost a hundred men—nothing but yellow-bellies
and weasels, under masks, scared white with their own sinning—

rushed the jailhouse here in Wytheville. (Just so you know what
kind of place this is, coloreds supposed to be joyous
just to strut these nasty cow paths call themselves sidewalks.)
Those hundred—you can bet I knew all of 'em—arced their
hateful selves over that sad milksop of a sheriff,

snatched keys, and stole my baby brother William from his
cell (*his* cell, like he had any choice in owning it).
Everybody—'cept for the colored folks—say our Will
killed that wild, no-'count Joe Heirt, who sure deserved his end
quick, by somebody's hand if not my brother's. Oh, and

in Wytheville, *everybody say* the same as *he did*.
They hung that poor chile from a beam in the mill, and while
he swung they took their shotguns and fired and fired into
that body that already wasn't William's body,
making sure it was dead like disappearing his head

wasn't enough. Next day, just like magic, nobody
knew who did anything. 'Cause they were everybody.
I've been trying not to slap the smug off their faces
ever since then. Smoke driftin' off their teeth when they smile.
They touch my shoulder, speak their slow shit, try on grieving.

William was a good boy, Sarah. He's sure gon' be missed.
But I'm my brother's only sister. I know my place
on the sidewalk. I keep fury away from my face,
away from my shuddering fists, and keep it knotted
inside, just beneath my everyday. There no one will
smell it. There it won't hurt anyone it doesn't know.

J.P. Silver

FORMERLY

POTTER & CO.   57 N. 8th St., Phila.

34

Down streets with names I thought I knew, the swift eclipse
of everything I was began so simply—old nags nosing
that creaking carriage toward the cemetery. It was August,
a damned blister of a day, but I wanted to follow
the dragged-out dirge on foot. I was a barren mother
sheathed in reams and reams of black, leaden cloth.
I wanted to stink like my dead son so that folks
lining the way—gaping, murmuring, pointing boldly
at my lusty collapse but not knowing a note of Caleb's
name—could sniff the acrid air and cough me into
disappearing. I mourned lurid, like someone without
language. Shoved all the way blue, I mourned with
my dragging stride, with snort and snot, with my spurned
curls smashed under a complicated hat. I wept wide
like an opened cage. I cried whole lying Bibles,
screeched the backsides of hymns. I heard someone
say *Lawd, that boy dead, she might as well be dead too.*
At his graveside, church folk held me back as I fought
to hurl myself into the damp mouth of his next mother.

Ten years on, the graves in Lebanon were robbed
of their dead. Negro bodies were piled high and carted
off in wagonloads so that bleached white amphitheaters
of bleached white men in bleached white smocks could
pull them apart in the name of stolen science. Caleb,

I assume your bones everywhere. I assume your heart,
carved thin and needled, refused them. I assume that
anything they couldn't kill again was shoved aside,
reckoned useless, thrown back in the direction
of mothers.

Their Story

She takes forever learning to read
the signs: she has no life outside of it.
She breathes so the child
may breathe. She should know
what a blessing there is in service.
She should know that she was
born to be drained,
the child to be filled.

> *My Story*
>
> I am nauseated by the thing—its mewing,
> its meek need, the beginning that so quickly
> veers to screech and claw. I have learned
> the perfect way to mimic cool love, cooing
> damnation while I cringe at its weight,
> its sour squirming heat on my legs.
> I sit on my slapping hand when a new tooth
> drives through the skin of my breast.
> Its first word—spat toward me—was the same
> name its gasping daddy calls out in the dark.
>
> How sweet of mister and missus to want
> this golden token of mammy and sweetums,
> cow and suckle. Cow honed the blade this
> morning. Cow needs to carve her given name
> into a new throat. But for now, Cow is content
> to doom us all with this one last stoic glimpse
> of me.

Unshuttered

You damn us with these stoic glimpses. You,
officially composed, gracefully caged,
you're girdled, stifled in your overdo
of buttoning and lace, so stiffly staged.
A waylaid rage, illuminated, can
become such softer fist within the held
and holding breath. Instead, the light—engaged
with cane, cravats, and corsets that retell
the body's mishap—blinds us to the hells
that seethe within your stare. You disappear,
dim gingerly to fray on a lapel,
and leave us with this dogged souvenir—
the ache for fictions etched in black and white,
our faces stripped by lies of shuttered light.

The past has done its awkward work. It rules
our now with such a feeble guarantee
while Jesus, azure-eyed, regrets His fools
still fixed on Northern stars. It hurts to be
your scions, sons from sons, your rumored free
and distant daughters, floundering in ways
that wound. And all you asked for was that we
never forget you were considered prey
before this dusty chic, or how each day
was conjured by your frenzied thirst for dawn.
Instead, your desperate stares are now arrayed
on shelves of shadowboxes, their warnings gone
to sepia and still. We hush your drum,
and hide behind whatever we've become.

When you were straightening your backs for us,
and fathoming our names, could you have known

how much escaping never ends? We must
grow canny to the chase, the metronome
dispatching of our children, dying prone
on streets with names you'd know. The swift eclipse
of sons and daughters, days that moan
beneath us like the burdened decks of ships—
as if we're following some hateful script
you prayed we'd never write. Back when you posed
and held and held your breath, waiting to slip
inside the clutch of flash—*Don't blink*—you froze,
captured a story that you knew we'd need,
a story we're just learning how to read.

Uncollected 2010–2024

Double Shovel on a Line from MLK's "Letter from a Birmingham Jail"

Prayers toward home, spat through your numb grizzle and fog, can't do what
long nights conjuring the fevered outline of a woman can do. No amens. Or else,

pray solid things like a plump canteen—pink shards of meat bobbing in a can
and poisons that move slow. The daydreamed hand that drags a crave—just one

thought, that one recollected touch, could drop you where you stand, it could do
long hurt to your measuring of days. There's nothing but rot at the end of *when*.

Think madhouse in the body, think on the plodding drown of the she and he,
letters returned, spritzed with heat that can't be reached. The way back to her is

long and all the roads are ocean. Want for solid things. If you're always alone,
write her name in needles on a deadened inch of your arm. Better to be shut in

than shut down, better backhanded than cracked wide, better a fool than a—
(Other men, triggered, beg you to slam shut your weep.) So stomp your narrow

cell, tally years, knit muscle even in your hands. Soon you'll find that other jail—
jail of the howling wolf, slow trample, jail of the crumpled Polaroid. In your cell—

narrow, bleached bright, scrubbed clear of sun—you've become a broken other,
a keyless trill, artist of all her mouths. Any man would rather be dead than

in love with clocks. *It's been 17 years, 17 years*, you write and write and write,
alone against a backdrop you keep managing to claw alive. Your life runs long.

Is the woman at least rattled by your long scribbled reach, all those letters
he probably reads to her, a new uncaged lover chuckling with bright pity? *Think*—

when was she last here, eyes locked on a space over your shoulder? How long
do you think you can leak all her silver and live? Shove your sorry thoughts

one last time toward *without*, then to *within*. To your left and right, men will and can pull their hearts from their chests. They will wallow with you in blue. Pray,

else you'll lose all you have—a man's way to be lonely as your life grows long. What you needed to know, your brothers knew. Women only live in prayers.

How to Find a Missing Black Woman

First, you'll have to notice that she's gone.
The sign could be a landscape, long wildflowered,
unbothered, scratched awake to secret a humbled body.
Or, obscenity on the shimmer of a river skin, a break
colored like struggle. A picture frame, askew in
the dust of an old Negro's shadowbox, shatters its
own glass and keens for her and keens for her, while
the outline of where she was turns slowly to chalk.
In a room, slapped to circus by neon from the street,
a man breaks in two over a bottle of brown liquor
and screeches a blues ballad to the fading sugar stink
of her neck. No one will remember anything or
anywhere she ever was, but she has cursed them
to walk different, that's how all over them she is.
Or was.

Walk backwards till you find a jukebox that still
swallows old money, listen to every record skip
from trying so hard to save her. You look behind
and beneath everything and see nothing. That chunk
of swine she had on low boil was strolled away
from and burned to firework, leaving behind a smell
like a backhand, leaving behind ashy babies with
unpicked hair and baffled bellies, leaving behind
a postdated rent check and a 'frigerator crammed
with souring, leaving behind her good job, leaving
behind her people staring into the void of where
she last laughed, leaving behind everything she had
to her name. Leaving behind her name.

You remember hearing that name, a country clutter
of syllables audacious as war, but now all you see
are cursive letters ghosting at their edges. Then you
don't even see that. She's gone when you see the air
wrenching and hissing to replace her. She's gone
because you refuse to see that she's gone. She's gone
because you never saw her. You see a back road
drawling slyly and picking its teeth. You see a tiny
disturbance in the earth. You see her picture when
you turn the page but you're always on the last page.
You see a dress crafted of black trash bags, with no
holes for her neck, her arms, her pretty plump legs.
There she is, gap-toothed and grinning on billboards
meant to blare directions for the good life. You see
her being a bad girl, probably responsible for
disappearing herself. You see empty. You see
a placard or two. Her name is wrong, and even
that is misspelled. You see no one everywhere.
You see the so-what of her, you see the ain't
of her. You see her gone girl. She's gone, girl.
What? No alert on X, not on FB, not on your IG.

Is someone missing?

Letter from Walpole

Sitting in my dimly lit cell
after having all my possession
confiscated from me,

In some places, a man owns only what
he can see. He can own a pummeled wall,
a sheet laundered until it dusts, a letter
groaning with olds and folds. He can
own a hoarded slab of bread, neon wads
of chewed gum, one curl-cornered
Polaroid of a small brown boy, or pages
from an old magazine scarred with
semen, water and soup. If he's lucky,
he also owns a squat jar of oil he uses
to grease his scalp and shine his dusty
knees. Even these are too many things.
What is owned by some men is owned
by other men. Some men are owned.

my loneliness demanded
that i disrupt my neighbor

How to tell if a black man is blue:

he stumbles into a lyric and never comes out

requesting something to read.

Letters tumbled and coaxed—he fought them in
his sleep until they nightmared to another nothing.
When he woke up, his mouth gaped wide
and pained, grappling with wound.

Which, in it self is a task,
in my repressive housing condition

Sometimes he forgets where he is.
He opens his eyes and thinks
I'll have my coffee first, but then
the smell of other men rides in
on a rancid wave and sways him,
all those caged bodies rising at once,
those few seconds they all believe

they are free

to receive anything from your neighbor
one must attach a solid object to a line
(torn sheet) and take direct aim
at the cell beside him.

And hope

And hope.

the line is close enough
to the two-inch opening
at the bottom of your door

to retract his line
and whatever else
that might be attached to it.

Which, in this instance
happens to have been
a poem
by you.

He used to think that poetry was all about
the longing for a woman, trying to put into
pretty words the good wrongs her body could
do, or maybe about rippling fields of flowers
in places he would never find himself. No one
had told him that a line of words could know
his name, that even his sinning had shape and heft,
and could line up nice on paper, just like that woman.

I was real impress
with your writing.
How you was able
to relate misfortunate and
articulate it on paper.

It took him hours sometimes, to scrawl
that list of all the ways he didn't fit,
turns he took that led him into alleys,
the women he regretted leaving, loving,
that thing his mama said he didn't listen to.
Sometimes it took him hours, but then
he had a list of what he'd done, and when
he looked at where he was, it all made sense.
He always heard men asking *why, why,*
and now he knew.

I also enjoy writing,
not particularly poetry,
but at times I find myself
needing to express
what I am feeling

What he is feeling—
a cracked aura. deep blue at 3 pm on a fuckin' Tuesday.
like sipping something clear and killing. mad at that roach
on his wall. but he won't kill that roach on his wall. forsaken
as a motherfucker. like crying into his mama's shoulder. like
standing up and walking out. like a whip right when it snaps.
like a poem.

and having no other outlet
other than my pen I create stories
that have a favorable senerio

which most of the time

help's ease my pain.

He thinks he'd be good in the movies, because
he writes himself into a laughter he can't stop.
He rides a horse, but doesn't shoot a gun. There
are no guns. He dances with a satin-wrapped
woman in a violent rain and doesn't get wet.
He writes himself a home, he writes himself
walls and a toilet that flushes, and he goes
from room to room and whoops, just to hear
somebody whoop back. He thinks he'd be that
good at life, so he writes himself one. He looks
so sharp when he steps inside it. But if there's
no one there but him, he steps outside again.
Revises the color.

At this time I am indigent
and have no one that would
purchase poetry for me.

If possible
please

        Please.

send
me
poetry

Nap Unleashed

In its beginning, earth was fractured, frail
with coveting, and could not wait for us—
so, flailing in the muscled clutch of grace,
we blessed this sullen place. As we were born
and born again, in tenements and lush,
exuberant savannas, flung from hips
of southern silver, lifted into life
while mamas shrieked and swore, as we were born
and born again, emphatic, snared within
our slap and wail, our breath already slowed
by blood's incessant question in our chests,
every dazzled witness rose to name
us yet again. The world was not prepared.
Inside its realm, no one could fathom us.

Inside its realm, no one could fathom us—
we brazen through their shuttered doors, we huge
inside their throats, we necessary storm,
our newborn crowns smeared flat with blood, so hot
against our little heads. The white mistake
was thinking that, once rinsed and blotted dry,
the clenched, rebellious snarl was simply hair
with nothing more to say. They saw instead
the way our skin corrals and guzzles sun,
our breathlessness, our legendary hips,
they saw what commerce needed them to see—
our backs grown wide and measured for the want
of work. They missed the hurricane of hair,
the springing from a thousand wicked roots.

That springing from a thousand wicked roots
was just the brash beginning, just the bray

of light that hisses warning—*Do not touch*
this hair, this vibing wire, these bellowed threads
of thundering, no, do not dare to poke
a prying finger into dark you do
not understand. Our hair is blade when we
decide that it should be—the fools who died
within its kink would speak of smother if
they could. Our hair is not your savior, not
your kumbaya, your ticket in. When it
began, so smashed and sleek with blood, we knew
that it had fist. Our hair can't be polite.
Once we were slaves. Our hair was furious.

Once we were slaves. Our hair was furious,
forever springing loose from plaits and bows,
rejecting homemade greases meant to tame
the wild and wiry bloom that snapped its bands
and leapt alive at every chance. At least
some part of us was running free, like flame
that hungers for a sky, like praying fixed
on someplace we knew heaven was. We sang
our songs but didn't move our mouths, we burned
to black inside ourselves. With rivers as
our mirrors, we began to build a wall
between our stolen air and us. We snapped
our dresses to our throats, made sure our hair
was braided thick against the spit of men.

Hair braided thick against the spit of men,
we hurtled forth—for years, we mystified
the whisper-tressed, but listened when they said
that we were wrong, not white or silk enough,
and that we'd never be unless we walked
into the fire, succumbing to a hate

we'd hoarded for ourselves. Because they loved
their blemished daughters, mamas twisted knobs
on cranky ovens, conjured flame, and made
us sit on rusted, wobbling kitchen chairs
beneath the ironing comb that charred our necks,
beneath the lye that chewed at scalp and root,
and we endured that hurt, forgot the days
our chaos crown had bellowed, nap unleashed.

Our crown still fought to bellow, nap unleashed,
though it was wounded, hammered down with heat
and oil that stank of animals and flowers,
although we wept while memorizing pale
and wispy heads in magazines. We gazed
and learned to suffer poisons to correct
our ugly, free us from the blunder of
ourselves. And as we listened, reaching up
to touch a stranger's head—a stranger head—
with strands that disappeared us, trapped us in
their strangling glamor, we remembered this—
that we are people destined to explode.
So we exploded toward ourselves again.

When we explode, we know ourselves again,
we shake our funky, liberated heads,
and raise our voices to the rafters—*Do
not dare touch these crowns.* And we are Accra,
and we are Alabama, Brooklyn, Watts,
and we are middle finger lifted toward
the seething witnesses to all this joy,
and we are Trinidad and Harlem, we
are bopping straight into the yesterday
we were, and straight into the history
we've made and straight into tomorrow with

our rampant naps so gleefully unchecked
so unrestrained, entwined 'til we become
a single soul, yet none of us the same.

A single soul, yet none of us the same,
we are the only government we need—
our vivid, cocky crowns stunned in their tilt
and swirl, they devastate and irritate,
they be our gospel, be our calling card,
they be our halo, be the way we reach
for sky. The crown is ours to snip or dye
a hundred awkward hues, it's ours to tuck
beneath a Sunday hat, to crimp and twist,
to scissor down to air, much like a man's.
This hair is all our other breath. It's art
upon our heads, a glory spill. It's wild,
bewildering and sexy in its snarl,
it's neon, razored, locked and knotted, looped

and neon, razored, locked and knotted, looped
and razored, locked and neon, looped and not
the business of just anyone, our hair
is blatantly political, a staunch
and blaring tangle, glory in our names,
the gospel on our bobbing heads, it's fierce—
and yes, still furious, still springing loose
from any peril set on silencing
its roar. You've underestimated us,
you didn't know the muscularity of kink
was busily rebirthing us—it taught
us all the ways to mouth our names
with Serengeti tongues, it's quarrelsome
and coiled, it's all the things but always black

and coiled. This hair is all the things. But, black
and wily goddesses, we've always known
the powerfulness of wearing our own sky,
the lyric of the scar, we've always known
that even though they dared to call us slaves,
we never were. If only they had heard
the freedom on our heads, the jubilant
triumphant wail of all that hair, its rude
unbridled verb, they would have left us free
to rule our own damned selves, to live our sweet
and colored lives. Our hair is throat, is knife
against the throat, is song within the throat,
it's how we rock and conquer every room,
our hair's the funk, the scorch, Aretha's growl

is hair, is funk, is scorch, Aretha's growl
is one of just a million ways the tale
is told. It's told in gospel hurtling toward
the rafters, told in warnings grunted blue
and deeper blue by Delta gals, it's told
in songs our mamas sang before they threw
those pressing combs into the fire. Go on
and raise your eyes to where we rise, go on
and hail the royalty we be, go on,
resent the ways we've vowed to live our souls
out loud. *But do not touch this hair,* the black
explode, the crowning of it all. Your hands
will never know a shelter in this heat,
so sweetly hellish on our perfect heads.

So sweetly hellish on our perfect heads,
this hair has known the yesterdays we know,
has lived the history we've lived. Once we
were slaves. And then there were the days we sat

on plastic kitchen chairs while trying not
to hear the sizzling iron comb, its teeth
intent on disappearing us. When they
were freed, embracing wild—each strand became
a fist that pierced the air, a strident voice
that sanctified and irritated, each
and every one its tiny god. You say
It's only hair, a consequence of blood,
a quirk of body. What it is is life.
And even history can't twist that truth.

Yes. Even history can't twist the truth,
can't warp the telling—see, our hair's the thing
that no one else will claim. It makes us like
nobody else. It seems there is a world
of silk, of blond and auburn, pinkish skin
that coppers under sun, but then
there's powerful nappy, there's the feral curl,
the everything there is, what black girls have
that no one else imagines. Mystery
prevails—it just may be the kiss of sun
that's braided in the braids, the moon that spits
12 its liquid light in dreaded ropes. The earth
was not prepared for what our locks would scream.
In its beginning, earth was fractured, frail.

In its beginning, earth was fractured, frail—
outside its realm, no one could fathom us,
our springing from a single wicked root.
When we began, our hair was furious
and braided thick against the spit of men.
Our chaos crown still razzles, nap unleashed,
and we explode, always ourselves again,
a single soul, yet none of us the same.

it's neon, razored, crimped and knotted, looped
and coiled, it's all the things but always black,
our hair's the funk, the scorch, Aretha's growl,
it's sweetly hellish on our perfect heads.
And even history can't twist this truth:
No woman wears the crown except the queen.

Pandemics

1

You once believed *it's only touch I want*
until what you were given was too much
of it—those toxic droplets drift and swerve,
infringing on your blood, corrupting it,
their needled clutch the same as murder.
It stuffs your lungs with mud and scrapes
your buckling throat with all its fitful blades.
The virus is a flood of mercy's absence.
In its lethal thrall, you pray in tongues
you swear are not your own, an angled moan
that mangles verbs you once assumed were God.
Lord I atone for my whole life, you say,
an outright lie that won't unlatch your breath
and teach it how to know the air again.

2

Alone with the sheer repetition, you turn
away from the pile of bodies, all the lost
and becoming gossamer, the fallen, spurned,
the unacknowledged, tubed and ventilated,
tossed to the hallway, Child, you will die
of counting the dead. They are in their silk beds,
beneath the wheels of patrol cars, crammed
in places we will never find them. There is
even one waiting for you at the end of your life.

3

You cannot open a door that has never been closed.
Don't misconstrue what is waiting for us. It is bigger
than breath. Someone will call you nigger this year,
same as the last, it won't even be whispered this time,

you will be reported for walking, for selling what you
own, for breathing toward the wrong subdivision,
for insisting upon your given name. In Long Island,
when they see you coming, two grown men will pose,
laughing, one with his knee on the neck of the other.
In Alabama, where your mother was born, a young girl
holds the sign BLACK LIVES SPLATTER and it will
look as if someone, maybe the girl, flung fun droplets
of red paint all over the placard and is proud of her
work because when the camera finds her, she grins,
goddamnit she grins, and again history binds your hands
before you can find the breath you need to slap her.

Practice Standing Unleashed and Clean

More than twelve million immigrants were processed through the Ellis Island Immigration Center. Those who had traveled in second or third class were subjected to a thirty-second health inspection immediately upon arrival to decide if they were fit to enter the United States. Often the examinations included the removal of all clothing, which was a foreign concept, especially for women. A check mark signaled a health problem that sent immigrants to the Ellis Island Immigrant Hospital, where they recovered or were kept until it was decided that they could not be cured and should be sent home.

Hide the awkward jolt of jawline, the fluttering eye, that wide
brazen slash of boat-burned skin. Count each breath in order
to pacify the bloodless roiling just beneath the rib, to squelch
the mushrooming boom of tumor. Give fever another name.
I open my mouth, just to moan, but instead cluttered nouns,
so un-American, spew from my throat and become steam
in the room. That heat ripples through the meandering queue
of souls and someone who was once my uncle grows dizzy
with not looking at me. I am asked to temporarily unbutton
the clawing children from my heavy skirt, to pull the rough
linen blouse over my head and through my thick salted hair.
A last shelter thuds hard, pools around my feet on the floor.

I traveled with a whole chattering country's restless mass
weakening my shoulders. But I offer it as both yesterday
and muscle. I come to you America, scrubbed almost clean,
but infected with memory and the bellow of broiling spices
in a long-ago kitchen. I come with a sickness insistent upon
root in my body, a sickness that may just be a frantic twist
from one life's air to another. I ask for nothing but a home
with windows of circled arms, for a warm that overwhelms
the tangled sounds that say my name. I ask for the beaten
woman with her torch uplifted to find me here and loose

my new face of venom and virus. I have practiced standing
unleashed and clean. I have practiced the words I know.

So I pray this new country receive me, stark naked now,
forearms chapped raw, although I am ill in underneath ways.
I know that I am freakish, wildly fragrant, curious land. I stink
of seawater and the overwrought moonwash I conjured to
restart my migrant heart. All I can be is here, stretched
between solace and surrender, terrified of the dusty mark
that identifies me as poison in every one of the wrong ways.
I could perish here on the edge of everything. Or the chalk
mark could be a wing on my breastbone, unleashing me
in the direction of light. Someone will help me find my clothes
and brush the salt from my hair. I am marked perfect, and
someone says heal in a voice I thought I brought from home.

The Price of the End of It

But now it's her stooped body in queue for the slab,
her blessed temperature you're fiddlin' with, and God's
holy directive shifts accordingly. Your mother holds
the tasteful funeral home brochures an inch from her
eyes until their horrible words unblur, shakes her head
at the insane cost of the gilded, pall-born tribute she truly
craves, asks again for whatever's cheap. May her Lord
forgive you as you just keep shuffling that cremation info
to the top of the pile. You remember how stupidly she
bobs her napped head to the wagging finger of God,
God again, always God, how resolutely she clutches
all the bluish notes in gospel—for her, "the fire next
time" is not a frugal means of disposing of soulless
shells, it is payback for a life clawed together outside
of her savior's cold little classroom. Oh, never you mind
the lesson she drilled into you after a handgun blasted
your father out of the world, what she said to end your
bouts of snot and fever, your worrisome new habits of
snatching tufts of hair from your own head and screaming
the onsets of dawn—Your daddy's not in that ol' body
anymore—and you unrolled your eyes just in time to look
that pliant, just in time to make her think you believed her.

Now that she has refused the neat conclusion of ash,
you are thinking of all the damned reams of paperwork
glorious ceremony requires, the feel of scrawling your
name over and over to officially end her. There will be too
many syrupy flowers draped over everywhere, the casket
lid flipped open, your oblivious mother's vaguely
whorish makeup job. You dread the hearse's eerie creep
through annoyed Ubers, the depressing pit, mourners
sneaking cell snaps, taking note of your absence of ache.

While this strange woman comparison-shops, zeroing in
on the pauper's special—Girl, what is a cloth casket?—
you remember years of screaming her name into a dead
phone after she scrubbed her whole history of your needy
little face. Now that she is frail and beholding, you should
demand that she answer for that kind of love. Or you
can love that way too. Go on. Throw a match into her hair.

Salutations in Search Of

1

Dear floaters, bloated kin. Dear flooded necks
and reckless leapers manic for the flow.
Though you are elegant in flight, your wrecks
distress the ocean's floor—the stark tableaus
of sliding skin and swarms of slither set
to drumbeat in your hollows. This is free
proclaimed by slaver's scourge—do you regret
rebutting scar with water? Dear debris,
that ocean mothers all your rampant funk
and spurts her undulating arms for you.
She likes to think that you are simply drunk
with purpose. Dear the voyage never knew
your name. You rise in pieces, loved to death,
at last unshackled. Time will hold your breath.

2

Dear wild tumultuous, your mouth. *Dear God.*
Your mouth, in fevered skirmish with the tongue,
denying sound for *rope* or *goldenrod.*
Dear mouth, still bulging with Atlantic, wrung
into its new. Your tangled words are lash
into the back, intending to explain
the gritted teeth inspected for a flash
of rot, the hefted cock or breast, a chain
that's wrenched away with clinging shreds of skin.
Dear going to market, beauty on the block,
seed driven deep. Dear chartered womb, within
you squirms a tendency. A paradox.
You trusted voyage, trussed to kin, and found
the tongue through tumult. Now you need a sound.

3

Dear mute contrivance, graceless drudge. Dear hexed,
Dear wily roots and conjures, Dear persist
with your existence—flaunting all that flexed
and bumptious brawn. Dear flagrantly dismissed,
the writhing in the cottonwood. Dear flail
and drip. Dear runaway who runs the hell
away. Dear prey for drooling cur. Dear veil
of Judas moon, its murmured decibel
of light. Dear cautious measurer of splay
and fury in a heedless star. (*Dear we.*)
Dear woman, who must now learn to unsay
her purpose as a mute machine. Dear be
that soft alive. Dear man, whose beating drum
was lost at sea. What nouns will you become?

4

Dear lurch and pirouette, Dear flamed facade,
Dear eye that won't dissolve. Your audience,
obsessed with shrinkage, fancies to applaud
and whoop, but damn—that eye, and the suspense
and dogged smolder of its wide-aloud.
Identified (of course) and doomed to swing,
you vow to witness. Your enraptured crowd—
delighting in your noosing as a thing
to do, do not wish to be seen by you.
Dear languid rhumba, freakish scorch and sway,
Dear blackened reckoning, Dear charred askew.
Dear stuff of nightmares seeping into day.
The fire has died—there's nothing of you there,
but they still see the fiction of your glare.

5

Dear Langston, Zora, Louis, Josephine,
Dear Harlem, their rampaging stanzas, still
explosive whether they are sugar-lean
pronouncements from a horn, the thrill
of stories touting faces like the ones
who hallelujah every time they read
themselves, or—not to be undone—
a pure astonishment of women. Need
this nurture and this verve on dimming days.
Dear give you back your name. Dear higher ground.
Dear noontime strutter, balancing pince-nez
and being Negro all upside that town.
Dear swinger to a thicker harmony,
Dear every man they said you couldn't be.

6

Dear migrant on a Greyhound, stunned upright,
or crammed into a wheezing Plymouth, or
bewildered by the rails soon to ignite
beneath your seat. Dear locked and shuttered door
with you on both the sides. Dear bound to be
more partial to the heat—folks say the chill
in ol' Chicago knows your bones. The key
is birthing your own sun and clutching 'til
it walks with you. Dear you, already done
surrendering magnolias, feigning shame
at chittlins, holding that amusing gun
to your own truant heart. Dear faultless aim,
Dear northern body scrubs at what it must,
that wily scarlet slap of southern dust.

7

Dear edgy citizen, Dear crazed careen
through multitudes of all the same as you.
Your skittish eyes outstretch. Dear seen
and then—as if on cue—unseen. You knew
enough to heed the itchy siren song
that cooed you through the rusty yawning maws
of factories. Dear often in the wrong
direction. Dear Chicago digs its claws
in you. The rank air gorgeous with disease
and pay stubs. Mayor Daley's startling swell,
his pocked and blustered face an odd reprise
of those you thought you left behind. Dear bell
that keeps on ringing—blues that hit their mark
and make you dance all righteous in the dark.

8

Dear still a nigger in all kinds of light,
Dear bullseye. Trees rise up on spindly toes
whenever all your skin strolls by. Dear quite
mistake of you. The way you dare expose
your neck and walk as if you own a thing.
Dear blue on you. And don't you wish there was
a ship, one chance to take a frenzied wing
into the ocean? Nothing but the buzz
of flashers pinning you against the past.
Dear suicide. Dear bullet in the back.
Dear in the headlights. You're not tagged to last
until the morning. You are tagged to crack
beneath their weight. And don't you dare believe
that any one of them will let you breathe.

9

Dear George, Trayvon, Breonna, Bree, Tamir,
Alatiana, Dominque, Jamel,
Antonio, DeAngelo, Romir,
Ashanti, Botham, Terence, John, Chanel,
Stephon, Philando, Kentry, Bee, Layleen,
Romelo, Emmett, Eleanor, Montay,
Jenisha, Kiki, Alton, Mack, Francine,
Tenisha, Eric, Dominick, Renee,
Michelle, Elijah, Nia, Amadou,
Akai, Monina, Cortez, Kentry, Sean,
Alberta, Michael, Gabriella, Lou,
Natasha, Brooklyn, Walter, Lee, Laquan,
Ahmaud, Mohamed, Elray, Aura, Shane,
Rayshard, Denali, Sandra, Oscar, Blane.

10

Dear someone who woke up without a son,
Dear damn the dawning. Echoes of a knock
with no boy crouched behind it, nothing done
to fix it. Dear reverberating shock,
Dear someone flailing, ripping at the air,
Dear hollow where he was. Dear someone who's
obsessed with resurrecting him, who dares
believe the muck of bullet hole and bruise
will ever breathe as anything but dead.
Dear someone loving body on its way
to being only body, just that red
and syrupy annoyance, hosed away
when street decorum says it will. Dear damn.
Dear chalk all washed to none. Dear traffic jam.

11

Dear woman wounded by the things you've heard.
Dear angry all your days, Dear vibing wire
on top your head. Dear better watch the words
you say to white folk—don't make them tired
of you. Dear wish you'd pinch those nostrils down,
that nose is half your face. Dear talk too loud.
Dear stay out the sun—you fool around,
get blacker than you are. What, you too proud
to settle for that ordinary man?
Gon' be too late real soon. Dear press
those naps. And don't you tell me that you plan
on yellin' 'bout that Black Lives Matter mess—
Dear who in the hell do you think you are?
Dear who in the hell do you think you are?

12

Dear someone who woke up without a sun,
and spun the blues—the singer moaned so hard
the record skipped to save itself. Dear done
so wrong. Dear fryin' lettuce in the lard,
Dear wonder could a matchbox hold your clothes,
Your child's been scraped up off the boulevard.
Since then, ain't seen yourself—do you suppose
some Rebel Yell can find you, hit you hard?
Dear someone who has chosen just to rust
instead of breathe—here's how they lied to you:
Your child will keep on dying, and you must
keep punching play to watch him blue and blue
until he trends. Then he's a photograph
who laughs at you and rips himself in half.

I rip another page in half.

Dear—

            Dear—

And start again.

Dear floaters, bloated kin, Dear flooded necks—
Dear wild tumultuous, your mouth. Dear God.
Dear mute contrivance, graceless drudge. Dear hexed—
Dear lurch and pirouette, Dear flamed facade—
Dear Langston, Zora, Louis, Josephine—
Dear migrant on a Greyhound, stunned upright—
Dear edgy citizen, Dear crazed careen—
Dear still a nigger in the neon's night—
Dear George, Trayvon, Breonna, Bree, Tamir—
Dear someone who woke up without their son—
Dear woman, wounded by the things you hear—
Dear anyone who wakes without a sun.

The Storefronts Wore Their Names

For those lost in the Tulsa Race Massacre, 1921

Lord, he was born a pesky question. Know
he always wore the danger hour of dusk.
The white folks named his skin impossible.
He teetered, balanced on the Negro inch
of sidewalks, dressed in hues of chance and mud,
eyes straight ahead, while trying to recall
the gospels that were conjured just for him:
Unsee the white men that you see. Demand
yourself upright. Your name is Rowland, give
it muscle. But in other mouths, that name
rode on their spit, and wrapped its muscled sound
around his neck. He barely found the breath
to ask what was so terrible in him.
Their answer always was some form of fire.

The answer's bound to be some form of fire,
perhaps a blinding spew of blood, a tree
with spindly arms that stiffen for the hang.
They sweat the need to disappear a thing,
to unbelieve in, unbecome a thing,
to call a man or boy a thing, to kill
all that he is until he's less than that.
The white man loves to torch a thing,
to torch a landscape flat, to turn it to
mistake but then deny it ever was.
They hate by hating most the things
they've made to disappear, but then
they see him walking, confident, unleashed,
his stride, too much a sin, the righteous flow

314

just like some Negroes stride, in overflow,
as if he were a man and white, he had
to realize how tight the anger wedged
inside their chests, and then—he touched the girl,
he ruined her sterling skin with his, they screeched
He touched the girl!, and if he did or not,
he did. And "touch," of course, meant he
had scraped her with his crave, he bit
and lapped and penetrated, he drew blood
and moan, he left that nigger sound on her,
a wail she'd always wear. He touched her. So
his rawboned throat was measured for the noose,
and white men gathered for his disappear,
their tangled voices rising like a pyre.

Entitled voices tangled in a choir
of loathing, bloated blue, its keyless shard
of song a bitter spitting of his name
again and yet again—he'd shortened it
to Diamond Dick, and yes, they were afraid
that might be right, afraid Miss Sarah Page
would fret and fever-flail, not wanting to
forget him happening to her. They named
him beast, and startled at the way that he
succumbed to cuffing—upright, bristling,
knowing his people just enough to know
they wouldn't let him swing, they wouldn't let
him disappear, his body left to those
who'd sing their privilege in place of dirge.

They warbled privilege because their days
were filled with nothing but deciding how
best to dispose of Diamond Dick, his blunt
and brutish fingers still an awkward source

of agitation for Miss Sarah Page,
who some folks thought might not recover from
that touch, or what she'd dreamed as touch. But they
had no real knowledge of the family
of Negroes, viscous as the stubborn blood
of Negroes, men who'd lay their own lives down
so he could live. He sensed their rumbling march
toward him, determined men who knew the sun
rose high on every man, so every man
deserved some sun. The homes, the offices,

were theirs to own. The storefronts wore their names.
And yes, they'd gathered, minds set on that boy,
not knowing if their numbers were enough
to save him from the rope, but needing to
be there, to say, *We're here*, to pull that boy
inside the widening circle of their arms,
to meet the menace in his jailers' glare
with menace of their own. And as they marched
in their unsettled silence, hefting sticks
and guns, their path ahead began to swell
with rancor, venom blurred the way, and soon
those bladed sounds for black rained down, that spit
in lieu of Christian names. The crackling in
the crowd, the screech of hate and all its ways

out loud. Those black men scrambled through the maze
of crowing throngs, that snarl, that sea of white,
the jail so close. And then—it could have been
most anything, so many things can push
"upstanding" men much closer to the monsters that
they are—a numbing shove, a rifle wrenched
away, the flinging of a barb that names
a man much less than what he is, the gall

of those who will not lower their eyes or step
aside, so many things can make a man
decide on blood, to answer questions no
one's asked with every form of fire. The boy
forgotten as that savage specter stalked
the streets of Greenwood—white men, taking aim.

On Greenwood streets, assured and laying claim
to everything a black man's hands had built,
the chosen ones obliterated all
the crooked triumphs, those unscrupulous
successes, lives that coloreds had been fool
enough to think were theirs to flaunt and mark
with their tenacious stain. A fever, dank,
relentless just below the skin, had wrapped
the white men in its blister. So they were
inclined to kill it all, to blast the breath
even from things that never lived. Their howl
was feral, and their hatred blind. The god
in them set out to touch their sacred flame
to everything they set their eyes upon.

In everything he set his eyes upon—
the riddled bench, the wretched rusting bars—
the captive boy saw shudder. Windows groaned
of endings. He had touched a white girl—he
had grabbed her arm to keep from falling, but
had gone and really touched the girl—and now
the much-debated sacrifice of his
one Negro body and its only neck
would never be enough. Even the air
was frantic soldier, slapping blue aside
to spew its heat. He heard the bullets
as they wounded wood in search of pulse.

He smelled the stigma in the brick, the ruin
of what he knew—those shelters built and blessed.

The place they loved, the shelters built and blessed,
their banks and offices, the barbershops,
the millinery with its smart chapeaux
and silken crowns for Sunday service, plus
the churches, where the congregations prayed
their shelters would be built and duly blessed,
the schools where children learned to write
their names, the corner shop where bolts of cloth
were cut for dresses, kitchens turned into
salons, that stink of flowery pomade
and burning hair. That place where music rose,
without a source or reason, mingling
with voices 'til the sky itself was song,
their tribulations waning with the dawn.

Their tribulations waned with every dawn
until the white man, so intent upon
his quaint possessions, rose to claim his dawn
again. He rose to claim his sky, his cloth
and nails, his wood, his bolts of silk, his shears
and pressing comb. He claimed his books, his pens,
the market and its crooked stairs, he claimed
the women, then the men, and then the black
in all their mirrors, then their mirrors.
And Greenwood, which was loved and built in search
of blessing, disappeared—gone was its whole
assembled soul, and all those loud black hands
were silenced, and were still. And were just hands.
Were silenced. And were still. And were just hands.

The men were silent, the women still. They just
unwound like time, wearing the worthless dust
of their dismembered homes, cloaking themselves
in folds of skin, just bulleted and brown,
no longer interesting, all that was left
was Negro, just the simple mud of it,
no lush brocade, chapeaux or bank accounts,
no, just the haughty scraps of wreckage,
that slaver bobbing in the distance, perhaps
a snippet of a chain. There, someone's hand.
A heart rifled to gone. And blood gumming
the soles of one man ambling, weeping.
He stopped—the path had crumbled and collapsed.
White man keep beatin' on that killin' drum.

They just keep pounding on that killing drum.
Inside his cell, Dick Rowland wondered if
his touching her had ended all the world.
All he could taste was red. He heard the screams
of colored men—brown liquor roar of them,
the muscled scrape, the sound that rattled earth
before it dimmed and drowned in psalm and blood.
The panicked one-note squall of children, and
the women—Jesus, Jesus, Jesus. But
he didn't hear one white man's voice, not one—
perhaps they'd died of too much carnage or
believed that they were God again. If so,
their craven clemency would save his life.
When you are born a question, you just know.

Whenever you are born a question, know
the answer's bound to be some form of fire.
Oh, how those Negroes strode, in overflow,
entitled, voices tangling in a choir

that warbled privilege as if their days
were theirs to own. And storefronts wore their names
out loud. Those black folks scrambled through the maze
of Greenwood streets, assured and laying claim
to everything they set their eyes upon,
to what they loved, to shelters built and blessed,
their tribulations waning with the dawn,
its silence, its still-rising. They found rest.
White folks kept beating on that killing drum,
too blind to know the hearts of those to come.

The Stuff of Astounding

A golden shovel for Juneteenth

Unless you spring from a smug and reckless history, unless
you've chosen to be blind to a ceaseless light, you see us. We
are shea-shined toddler writhing through Sunday sermon, we are
grizzled elder gingerly unfolding his last body. We are intent
and insistent upon the human in ourselves. We are the doctor on
another day at the edge of reason, coaxing a wrong hope, ripping
open a gasping body to find air. We are men dripping from the
burly branches of young trees, breathing last love for a world

both foreseen and absurd. What reason can we conjure from
suicides of the cuffed, the soft target of the black back? In its
rhythmic unreel, time keeps including us, even as our aged root
is doggedly plucked and trampled, cursed by ham-fisted spitters in
spasms of blinding white. See how we push on as enigma, the
free out loud, the audaciously unleashed, how slyly we scan the sky—
all that wet voltage and scatters of furious star—to realize that we
have been gifted an ancient grace. No, we didn't begin to live

when, on the 19th June day of that awkward spring, we heard—with
no joy, monotone flecked with disbelieving—*Seems you and these
other ones are free.* There was no beginning in that moment. Our truths—
the ones we were birthed with—had already met reckoning in the
fields as we muttered tangled nouns of home. We reveled in black
from there to now, our rampant hue and nap, the unbridled breath
that resides in the rafters, from then to here, everything we are is
the stuff of astounding. We are a mother humming shards of gospel

into the silk curls of her newborn, we are the harried sister on the
elevator to the weekly paycheck mama dreamed for her. We are black
in all the ways there are—perm and kink, upstart and elder, juke voice,
testifying whisper. We'll heft our clumsy homemade placards, we will

fold in the gloom, snot-weeping to a bladed blue song. But we will not be what those who crave us chained define as free, we will not be grateful for the taint of their tenets. We will not be beholding or silent as we're gifted a sliver of the America we built—because we own the

stink and hallelujah of it, its burden and snarl, its bodacious black and otherwise. Only those feigning blindness fail to see the body of work we are, the work of body we have done. Everything is no less than what it is because of us. None of us believe that free fell upon us like some man-made blessing, granted by a signature and an abruptly opened door. Listen to the thousand ways we say black out loud. Hear a whole people celebrate our brief, untethered lives, then find your own place inside our song. Make the singing matter.

To Little Black Girls, Risking Flower

And then day came,
when the risk
to remain tight
in a bud
was more painful
than the risk
it took
to blossom.
      —Anaïs Nin

Blossom when you're ready, but rough. Be quaint explosive. And
to those who spoke you dim, dismissed your shade of green, then
took your imagination for manic romps in the drizzle—the
it they mistook for weather was too cartoonish to spoil the day.

Risk the lush you've never seen. Forget how winter first came—
the unrhymed shudder, the gray dressed like your father; when,
thanks to the loud religion of wind, you couldn't find your face, and the
painful trick of season moved through you like a knife of ice. Risk

more. Risk smolder. Risk blood flower. Risk voice. (Like you, it too
was often just storm not knowing why.) Risk is why you remain,
bud like an opening hand, sprouting your mere devastation of tight
aroma, why you'll strut thorn, sink flytrap canines into bland satin,

into a landscape of concrete, unloosing the notion of grass. What a
tight-clenched jubilation you are, what a plump thirsting bud,
remaining unswerved in your reach for any sky. If your aim was
to unfurl, terrify, sparkle with damage, you'll do that and more.

Risk lurks in every inch of soil as frost or scorch, and it's painful the way soil can stunt the upward it insists upon. You're more than when you were just a whimpering mistake beneath the dirt, the camellia clawing for first breath. Risk that breathlessness. Risk

day, risk slap of sun, risk yawning wide, risk the itch and choke of it, the damned wheel of days, growth and all the dirty water it took. Then be that quaint explosive. Growl out with howling, red vibrato, and own everything weather had done to you. Blare, girl. Blossom.

What Daughters Come Down To

For what I'm sure is the fifth time, my mother
plugs in a flat mournful hum where the words
I love you too should be. Then she hangs up

without saying goodbye. I squeeze my eyes
shut, try to imagine 82 autumns in the bones,
in her rasping joints, in the cool, jaded thump

of what is still a migrant's ever-arriving heart.
However, I believe she is required to love me.
I wonder what God was teaching her all those

years, those day after days coaxing raucous
hips into deadening girdles and gray A-lines
so she could lose her damned mind to organ.

Was it all theater, a screeching of north when
south was what itched her, all of it mock belly,
the nails, splinter-spewing cross, some sly

spirit habitually overloading her spine, making
her dance thirsty and unfolded? How could all
those wry hymns and hot-sauced hallelujahs

lead to this hum, clipped connect and hush?
I am hundreds of miles away, but I can see
where she is sitting, hand still on the phone.

Every surface in her tiny apartment is scoured
and bleached, draped in a disinfectant meld
of rainshower and blades. The kitchen glints.

Jesus' searing blue eyes look down on everything.
Her rugs are faultless. The purpled tulips I
have sent for her birthday are insistent feral

beauty, a blood in the room. Like her daughter,
they have bloomed in the clutches of vapor.
I love you too, she thinks out loud, but can't.

70

But she was learning to love moments. To love moments for themselves.

—Gwendolyn Brooks, *Maud Martha*

Well first, it seems immeasurably unjust
that no one clues you to this bombshell—you
will lose your pubic hair! No one brought up
this grave development, the swift debut
of silver slowly turning soulless gray,
then just an anarchy of wire, 'til one
by one, your glistening strands betray
you, disengage and drift. Behold and lo,
you're bald in undreamt ways. My perfumed kink
and curl, dense lace embellishing the door
to everything, no longer shines its light
for episodic visitors. I own
a home not quite abandoned, simply stripped,
the fireplace still ablaze within its walls.

I'm shamed by how much satisfaction I
experience when I scan random crowds
and whisper *Everyone I see will die.*
The difference now is that I'm well aware
that I'm included. If I shut my eyes
to sleep, to hush this drowsy body down
because the world is swirling, when I wake
I'm just a little farther underground.
And yes, I'm terrified, and so are you,
admit it. Someone said you die and just
relive the life you've lost, again, again,
again, with all its woe and wounds. *That's* hell.
I think I'd rather ceaselessly replay
that breathing just before the end of breath.

I mourn the many poems that I failed
to write, and then those poems that I failed—
the poems I assumed would shove a life
back into life, unlatch a cage or turn

a thousand thirsty bullets back around,
revive a fallen daddy, shrink a war,
unreeling lines I thought could heal a thing,
slam shut a thing, reverse a thing or teach
an Annie Pearl to love her reckless child.
I grieve the lawless verses that fought back
and silenced me because I lacked the spine
required to know the tale they told was mine.
I trusted myself blind. I really thought
the words would grow to gospel in my hands.

And back to death again. It hovers, smirks,
and rides that vile McRib right to my mouth
and down. It's eyeing me. Who'll greet me at
the gates? A God? No God? I've seen the hope—
resuscitated Woofs and Fluffys, kin
now tumor-less and gleeful, those
who raised you younger than they ever were
all hauling ass through heaven toward you.
My daddy, with his glinting golden mouth,
and Brady Bear my Berner, Ron the mutt,
and yes, my mother, maybe with a heart
that works. This Hallmark paradise does
what a blindfold does—you crave a light
that isn't there until it is. It's not.

But what about the rampant blaze that scars
that other place? Incendiary claws
that fight to pull you down? Most poets swear
they've been to hell, prefer the place because
there's no gap left for silence, there's no time
to muse, regret, revise or wonder what
you've done or haven't, just the bellowing
of flames that shift your skin. The baying of
Beelzebub begins and keeps beginning.

But I suspect this too is trickery—
a candy dangled, daring poets near.
We don't mind fire if there's a tale attached.
But what of me, whose greatest fear is dirt
and stillness? What if now is what there is?

For what must be the thousandth time, I watch
the shudder-hipped industrious machine that is
Beyoncé's body and it's like I'm on
another planet. When you're 70,
it's best to file that under "kiss my old
decrepit ass" and go about your biz.
So what's life like? Let's see. I move,
a sound comes out—a yowl, a groan, a pained
unwinding hiss. Or if it's just my knee
again, a scream that freaks the birds outside.
My neck is prone to locking, and my eyes
can only work behind a nerdy chunk
of thick prescription glass. And oops, it time
to wind this sonnet down, but there is soooo

much left to gripe about, so let's proceed.
I stare at my reflection, and I see
my melody is waning—no surprise,
but only blues take root and hold. I spot
inside myself the girl who never was
less than a dance, who loved her daddy like
a god. I wallow in my history
because there's just so goddamned much
of it. And then I wonder if I've done
enough. Or anything. I question me
until I have sit and catch my breath.
Oh, hallelujah all this old. It's what
I've done. I wrote, I loved, I broke apart.
I write. I love. I break apart.

Scars Poetica

Today, Los Angeles is claws of seething copper, the air
ashed and callous. While the sweep of it smolders, I
learn that Paris Hilton has lost her home. Meanwhile,
in Altadena, Black folk rake through cinder for remnants

of worship, brittle papers that insist they are who they are,
or any pocked porcelain from grandmama's shadowbox.
The holocaust feeds the rampaging theory that the earth
is shutting down, spurning the pageant of her own murder,

mapping out yet another plan to blast her ruined body
clean of us. Look at her, buck naked to the sun's animus,
riverbeds torrid. Her ether is choked by fracked gas,
spurting Mustangs and Subarus, droplets of human shit.

She is weary of the bright prickle of warfare on her skin,
and the vapid who claim her as mother while cackling
at prophecy. When the earth exhausts her savagery on
oceans, crumples interstates or torches subdivisions flat,

she risks stopping her own heart. Blind to that selflessness,
we go about the stony-faced business of offing ourselves
and each other. We liquify neat rows of first-graders
with cartoonish firepower, dismember spouses, strafe

hospitals and churches, leave crusted toddlers roped
to radiators, hurl our inexpressible sadness from rooftops
and windows. Our hate has muscle. Vexed by not-our
version of deity, we knife believers, topple and shatter

their emblems. We kill without blinking, loathe without
thought. You can be too wrong to merit the thud in your

chest, too suddenly wrong for the everywhere air. And
if we are not the killed or killer, or both, it is the theater

of dying that consumes us. Copy/paste that url, click that
key, see Walter Scott's back implode, on loop. See Mamie
Till slump at the sight of her battered, ashen son. Watch
the exuberant procession, until suddenly the revered head

of Jackie's husband bursts and flecks her skirt. Feel that
knock on the door, hear that phone call, read that text
again and again. See Jonestown and Tulsa and Auschwitz
and all 270 minutes of Michael Brown's body sprawled

on Canfield Street under an apathetic August. Listen as
Eric Garner pleads and pleads for the simplest thing. Click
more keys and watch a rabid circle of streamers urging
a timid boy to blade his wrists while they cheer him on.

On the F train in New York, a woman was set on fire.
Click for the photo. She stands in the train car, sways
like a bone-tired commuter, fully aflame, alone. It was
decided that the controlled burn was best. All I am is

poet. I am small, just one enfeebled fist, a whimper
beneath the weight. I am seventy years of witness that
poetry can change your life, but changes nothing else.
No unleashed havoc calms to my quatrains, no ghazal

coaxes our earth from her cliff's edge. I write because
it's contrary to kill. Because *anemone* sounds the way
it does. I write because George Floyd cried out for
his dead mother. I write because she answered him.

acknowledging

there isn't one of you i *shouldn't* thank
or marvel at your presence in this life—
if you are reading this, then there's no doubt
you've visited as muse, you've strode as wraith
throughout my lines, you've wept with me or you
have granted shelter. some have cursed my path
or grinned so slyly that i never felt
the entry of the knife—you too have led
to poems, stern tercets that couldn't evade
those conjured nouns, the sting of music.
I feel I must have lived a thousand lives
with all of you as witness to the bliss,
the ruin, the messes I mistook for love,
the slap of loss, a father who won't sing
again, the rampant happy, spittle on
the mic. To all of you stomped the stage
and faced a room of strangers, sweating while
they scrawled your poem's worth on poster boards
then lofted scores for everyone to see
(although, as Allan Wolf was known to say,
"The points are not the point.") Oh, holy Chi,
where everything began—the Get-Me-High,
then Neutral Turf, and yes the Mill, that screech
of neon green, and all those shredded dripped
brassieres as quaint decor while Patsy Cline
went crazy on the juke, my overload
of love for Marc, the grizzled genesis
of mayhem that continues to this day,
no matter who screams otherwise. Of course,
there's Michael Warr, who grabbed my hand
and led me straight into the storm,
and Cin, and Dean, and Lisa B, the Anns

(both Kurt and Bang), Lombardo, Marty, Weeds
at fifteen fifty-five, with oceans of
tequila gushing from the faucets in
the john, Gregorio in charge, and Serge,
who only wrote two poems in his life—
in sixth and seventh grade. Hey, Windy Cit,
I owe you everything for all of this,
inside the slam and out, although the spark
was Luis asking if I had a book
and Tia Chucha waiting in the wings.
Then all those Saturdays, me shelving books
at Guild, and Lordy, Madame Brooks strolls in—
I thank this life for her (and for the blurb!),
to avery, Tugg, Haki and Angela,
and Andrea, EmRose and Nora Brooks
(the daughter of beloved Mama Gwen),
Tyehimba Jess, a mastermind of sound,
a monster on the harp, who had my back
from Chi to CSI to right here where
we stand. The Poetry Foundation and
Portillo's, Lou Malnati's, Sharon, Rick,
and Roger, Madison and Kedzie, dogs
with never ever ketchup, Wrigley Field,
and Schurz. But who said that Chicago was
the first and last and all of it? I can't
forget the Nuyorican, Holman and
Miguel, Cornelius, Toi and Cave.
Amanda and Mahogany, and Jive
who always spins Atomic Dog for me,
the Cantab with its fragrant john
and Judy slinging toxins 'hind the bar,
and Lord, *the poems.* All my sugarlumps—
Danez and Paul and Sam and Hieu,
Saeed, Safia, Fatimah and all

my students—Princeton, CSI, the crew
at Stonecoast, SNC (I love you, Bri),
and every workshopper from Ghana to
Dubai. MacDowell, Civitella, and
the bats at Yaddo. Guggenheim and Tufts,
and Zoland, Coffee House, Northwestern and
my brand-new folks at Scribner. Everyone
who jammed at Prince's Purple Poetry
soiree. And Benjamin B. Busch, *you said
it,* several times, before I learned to say
it to myself. And I love you for that.
At last, my coven—Carolyn, Suzanne,
Ilyse, Sholeh and Di, Susan and Lynne.
Hey sisters, you remember what we vowed
upon the shore as we were saying goodbye?
The ocean heard, and it will not forget.

About the Author

Patricia Smith is an inductee of the American Academy of Arts and Sciences and the recipient of the Ruth Lilly Poetry Prize for Lifetime Achievement. She is the author of nine acclaimed books of poetry, including *Unshuttered* (2023); *Incendiary Art*, finalist for the 2018 Pulitzer Prize and winner of the 2018 Kingsley Tufts Poetry Award, the 2017 Los Angeles Times Book Prize, and the 2018 NAACP Image Award; *Shoulda Been Jimi Savannah*, winner of the Lenore Marshall Poetry Prize from the Academy of American Poets; and *Blood Dazzler*, a National Book Award finalist. A Guggenheim Fellow, a National Endowment for the Arts grant recipient, a finalist for the Neustadt International Prize for Literature, and a four-time individual champion of the National Poetry Slam, the most successful poet in the competition's history. Smith is a creative writing professor in the Lewis Center for the Arts at Princeton University and a former distinguished professor at the City University of New York. She lives in New Jersey with her husband, the novelist Bruce DeSilva, her granddaughter Mikaila, and her beloved doggo, the Mistress Wrigley Field.